Unless otherwise indicated, all Scripture quotations are taken from the *King James Version* (KJV) of the Bible.

All rights reserved. No portion of this book may be reproduced, stored in a retrieval system, or transmitted in any form or by any means - electronic, mechanical, photocopy, recording, scanning, or otherwise - without prior written permission of the author.

Transcribed by Diane Narlock
Edited by Brad Shirley

Copyright © 2012 Dr. Leonard Gardner
All rights reserved.
ISBN-10: 1481086464
ISBN-13: 978-1481086462

Treasures in the Word

Volume 1

Dr. Leonard Gardner

2012

Treasures in the Word
Volume 1

Contents

Introduction 1
Genesis 1:1-5...Darkness and Light 5
Genesis 1:1-27 The Kingdoms... 7
Genesis 1:26-28...The Giver 8
Genesis 4:1-5...Cain and Abel 9
Genesis 6:19-21...Food in the Ark 10
Genesis 9:20-21...Drunk on Success... 12
Genesis 17:1-15...The Covenant Name 12
Genesis 27:21-23...Follow What You Hear, Not What You Feel 13
Genesis 28:11-12...Ascending and Descending 14
Genesis 35:18-19...We Are Who Our Father Says We Are!......................... 16
Genesis 37:31...The Coat of Many Colors 17
Leviticus 16:1-22...The Scapegoat.. 18
Numbers 21:8-9...Motives and Worship 20
Ruth 1:14...Kisser or Cleaver?.. 23
I Samuel 10:1...Anointed by Man or God?... 23
I Samuel 17:26-46...Focus on God, Not the Giant 24
II Samuel 6:16...Looking Through a Window 25
II Samuel 24:24...There is a Cost.. 26
II Kings 4:2...Never Without Oil 27
II Kings 6:1-7...The Cutting Edge 27
II Chronicles 24:14...The Purpose of the Vessels 28
Song of Solomon 6:1...Keeping Our Own Vineyard 29
Song of Solomon 1:9...Pulling the King's Chariots..................................... 30
Song of Solomon 2:9...Like the Hart 32
Isaiah 10:27...Breaking vs. Destroying the Yoke... 34
Isaiah 40:2...Giving the Double 35
Isaiah 43:2..."When" and "Through".. 36
Jeremiah 12:5...It's Harvest Time 37
Jeremiah 18:1-2...Knowing What He Means 38
Ezekiel 3:1-3...Delivering the Word with the Right Spirit.......................... 39
Daniel 3 and Daniel 6...Delivered In the Trial, Not From It 41

Joel 2:28-32…We Need Everyone! 42
Haggai 2:18-19…The Power in the Seed 43
Zechariah 13:1...A Fountain Opened 45
Malachi 4:6 and Revelation 22:21...Curse vs. Grace 47
Matthew 10:5-14...Handling Rejection..47
Matthew 13:44...It's OK to Teach It Again! 49
Matthew 13:44...Buying the Whole Field...50
Matthew 17:24-27...We Don't Have To, But We Will....................................51
Matthew 18:1-6...Become As This Little Child 53
Matthew 21:6-7...We Must Deal with the Flesh 54
Matthew 23:12…Humility..55
Matthew 25:1-13…Are You Sleeping? 56
Matthew 26:53...Twelve Legions of Angels 57
Matthew 26:74-75…A New Beginning 58
Matthew 28:19...Go Ye..58
Matthew, Mark, Luke, and John…Different Perspectives 59
Mark 4:35-41…Taking a Test 60
Mark 5:25-34…They Said, He Said 62
Mark 8:22-25...Seeing Men as Trees 65
Mark 15:22…The Place of a Skull 67
Luke 1:31…The Father Knew the Mission...68
Luke 1:46…Rejoice in the Promise 69
Luke 2:7…Laid in a Manger 69
Luke 6:6-11…Signs and Healings 71
Luke 6:36-38...The Law of Reciprocity..73
Luke 9:51-56...Don't Proof-Text! 74
Luke 10:17-19…Serpents and Scorpions 75
Luke 15:11-32…The Father's Love 76
Luke 15:11-32…In the Family but Not in the House 78
Luke 15:11-32…Six Signs of Unforgiveness 78
Luke 17:11-19…Jesus Wants Us To Be Whole! 81
Luke 19:1-10...Who is the Greater Sinner? 84
John 1:1-5...Darkness and Light 85
John 1:23...A Voice, Not an Echo 86
John 1:37-42...A Stone and the Rock 87
John 1:51…Verily, Verily 88
John 2:1-11...Following Mary's Example 89
John 4:1-42...Jacob's Well 90
John 5:1-16...Lacking Power 91
John 8:2-11...Case Closed! 93
John 11:44...God Allows Us to Participate in His Miracles 95
John 12:1-11...Don't Let the Thief Take Your Gift 97

John 20:1-10...The Lesson of the Folded Napkin 98
John 21:15-17...Love and Relationship 99
John 21:15-17...Feeding and Nurturing the Lambs... 100
Acts 3:1-11...The Importance of Discipleship 101
Acts 13:22...A Man After God's Own Heart... 102
Acts 28:1-5...Shake the Serpent into the Fire 103
I Corinthians 9:25-27...Out to Pasture 104
Ephesians 4:15-16...Every Joint Supplies... 104
Philippians 4:8...Before We Think or Speak 106
Philippians 4:11-19...Christ's Strength and Supply 107
Colossians 1:12-13...Darkness and Light 109
II Timothy 3:12...Suffering Persecution 109
II Timothy 4:7...I Have Finished My Course... 110
Hebrews 8:5...Go to the Mount... 111
Hebrews 8:12...He Chooses Not to Remember 113

Introduction

The inspiration for this book came from the remarkable account of Ruth, Naomi, and Boaz in the Book of Ruth. It was barley harvest time, which was significant in Palestine because barley was the most popular and prevalent cereal among people that were poor. Barley is a seed that can endure the heat without perishing.

A good man named Boaz went into his fields to examine the harvest when a young lady named Ruth caught his attention and found favor in his eyes. Ruth was a woman of strong character who had committed her life, at great personal sacrifice, to care for (feed, nourish, and nurture) her mother-in-law Naomi. In fact, Ruth had left her country and her home in order to commit herself to the well-being of Naomi. Upon seeing Ruth's commitment, Boaz' heart was moved, and he effectively said to his servants, "As you're walking among the barley, I want you to drop handfuls of plenty along the way so the young woman can pick them up and do the very thing that is in her heart to do - feed and care for her mother-in-law. Furthermore, whenever she is thirsty, don't require her to go all the way back to Jerusalem to get water. Instead, let her drink of the water you have drawn so that she can continue her work."

As the Lord began to open this story to me, I saw myself occupying the role of a servant in the field of Boaz (who is a type of our Lord). I sensed that my task was to prepare to drop handfuls of plenty which the Lord had blessed me with over the years so that the "Ruths" of today, (leaders, pastors, Sunday school teachers, and anyone responsible for feeding others spiritually) can continue to be effective in the feeding of the "Naomis" that God has placed in their care. Therefore, the entire purpose of this book is to "feed the feeders." My deep desire is to drop a few "handfuls" along the way for you to pick up. I pray that you will be blessed and encouraged so that you will, in turn, feed others.

My purpose in writing this book is simply to bless you so that you can bless others. As you read through the many "handfuls" of Biblical truth in this book, which I call "Treasures in the Word," if one nugget of truth doesn't particularly resonate with your heart at that time, simply let that handful lie there and move on. Perhaps it will be meaningful to someone else. As a pastor for many years, I know how important it was to me to discover treasures in the Word that I could preach to my congregation. I recall going into Bible bookstores and searching the shelves for a book that contained what I considered to be inspirational keys, nuggets, seeds, or treasures that I was hoping the Holy Spirit could explode in my heart and which could be the basis for a powerful and anointed sermon. Sadly, I frequently left the bookstores disappointed.

Throughout the decades of pastoring, I attended many conferences and conventions and came away blessed and encouraged. However, even after attending tremendous gatherings of believers, I often went home burdened with the sobering reality that I had to preach the next morning, and with the desperate desire to preach a fresh and "alive" message to the people of my congregation. It was at times like those that I would have appreciated a book such as this one. I trust that "Treasures in the Word" will provide you with handfuls of truth that the Lord will quicken to your heart. I pray that the treasures in this book will make a difference in your life and ministry, and will be a blessing to you and a source of strength. I'm your fellow laborer, a servant who will be grateful if I can drop something along the way that will be a blessing to you and the people to whom you minister.

Before we begin to delve into some of the treasures in the Word, please know that I believe in the inspiration of the entire Bible, both the Old and the New Testaments. I only say this because there are some today that suggest perhaps "old" means outdated. That is incorrect! "Old" simply means "former." Therefore, we'll be extracting treasures from both the former and latter covenants. I believe the Bible is different than any book that has been written by man. Books written by humans contain what we call "filler words," which are words that make the reading more palatable and the transitions smoother. The Bible contains no such "filler" words. <u>Every</u> word is important and inspired by the Holy Spirit.

Speed reading instructors teach readers to identify and read only key words and move rapidly over the words that are not significant. However, it is a tremendous mistake to try to "speed read" the Bible because as I stated above, <u>every</u> word in the Bible is important. Jesus declared in Matthew 4:4, "Man shall not live by bread alone but by <u>every</u> word that proceedeth out of the mouth of God." II Timothy 3:16 states, "<u>All</u> scripture is given by inspiration of God." I believe that the mention of numbers and proper names of people and places are very significant. We should not simply "read" the Bible; we should study it and meditate upon its truths. The Bible itself never instructs us to <u>read</u> the Bible - it states that we should <u>study</u> the Bible. 2 Timothy 2:15 states, "<u>Study</u> to show thyself approved unto God, a workman that needeth not be ashamed, rightly dividing the word of truth." I believe that God is pleased when we carefully study His Word.

Proverbs 25:2 states, "It is the glory (this word means 'privilege' in the Hebrew language) of God to conceal a matter, but the honor of kings is to search out a matter." I believe that is the way the Lord wants us to treat His Word. He wants us to immerse ourselves in the Word, and as we study, the Holy Spirit quickens the Word to our hearts. When we spend time in the Word, we should not move on until the Lord ministers in a fuller, greater way the truth(s) that He desires to deposit in our heart.

I say this as an introductory statement because this book, "Treasures in the Word," takes a slightly different approach than a typical Christian book, and may present things differently than you may normally hear when someone preaches or teaches. When we hear a sermon, we expect continuity between sentences and some sort of progressive thought process helping to develop or clarify a truth or topic. This book is different in that we will "bounce" from one scripture to another and the two adjoining subjects may not seem closely connected. Please keep in mind that my goal with this book is not to present or develop one central theme or one scriptural truth or topic, but rather to simply drop some handfuls of truth "here and there" so you can pick up what the Holy Spirit quickens to you.

The Holy Spirit helps us to build around a nugget of truth, but trying to build a message without that nugget is like slicing bologna with a spoon. We need the nugget to build around! When a nugget of truth is alive in your heart and you develop it and then proclaim it with passion and conviction, it is a tremendously powerful ministry experience.

Let's begin our walk through the harvest field as we pick up handfuls of treasures in the Word!

Genesis 1:1-5...Darkness and Light

In speaking of heaven, Revelation 21:25 declares, "....for there shall be no night there." In heaven, there will be no darkness and no night! It will be light forever and ever. I have observed in the Scriptures that every time God works in any way, He always ends in the light. He always dispels the darkness and ends in the light, just like He will ultimately do at the end of time, because in eternity, there will be no more darkness according to Revelation 21:23-25.

This principle is not only found at the end of the Bible, but also at the very beginning! Genesis 1:1-2a declares, "In the beginning God created the heaven and the earth. And the earth was without form and void."

The Hebrew word translated "was" in that verse is more accurately translated "became." This same Hebrew word is translated "became" sixty seven times in the Bible and is translated "came to pass" five hundred five times. Therefore, we can accurately read this verse in this way: "And the earth <u>became</u> without form and void and darkness was upon the face of the deep. And the Spirit of God moved upon the face of the waters. And God said, Let there be light; and there <u>became</u> light." Therefore, there <u>became</u> darkness...then God spoke and there <u>became</u> light.

Genesis 1:5 states, "And God called the light Day, and the darkness he called Night, And the evening and the morning were the first day." The evening and the morning were the first day. The ordering of the words in that verse is interesting, because we typically see things the other way around, but we actually have it backwards. We think the morning and the evening were the first day, in that order. We believe that the morning preceded the evening, but that's not what the Bible says! The evening and the morning were the first day because <u>God ends everything in the light</u>.

Dr. Leonard Gardner

Genesis 1:1-27 The Kingdoms

Genesis 1:1 begins with, "In the beginning God..." If we cannot believe the first four words of the Bible, there is no reason to read any further. We must, first and foremost, know and understand that God has always existed and will always exist, and His kingdom has always existed and will always exist. He is the Creator, the eternally existent One. In addition to His eternal kingdom, God created other kingdoms which are lower in hierarchy in relation to His kingdom and subservient to His kingdom.

Genesis 1:11-13 describes the work of God on the third day of creation when He spoke the <u>plant kingdom</u> into existence. Genesis 1:20-25 describes the fifth day when He spoke the <u>animal kingdom</u> into existence, and Genesis 1:26-27 describes the sixth day when God created the male and the female, or the <u>human kingdom</u>.

We must understand that there is a clear difference between the kingdoms. God created the kingdoms separately, and a member of one kingdom cannot "evolve" into a member of another kingdom. In the hierarchy, the lowest kingdom is the plant kingdom. The next higher is the animal kingdom. The next higher is the human kingdom, and the highest of all is the eternal Kingdom of God.

Think about this truth for a moment...<u>*nothing in a lower kingdom*</u>

can become a part of the higher kingdom except by death. A plant cannot become part of an animal unless it dies. The cow goes out in the field and eats the grass. The grass becomes part of the cow because the grass died. And, when we eat beef, the meat that we ingest becomes a part of the human kingdom because the cow died.

However, when we take one step further up the hierarchy to the human kingdom, we discover a problem, because through our own death we can't become a part of the Kingdom of God. Therefore, God who so loved the world became a part of the human kingdom (the Incarnation of Christ) and <u>He</u> died that we humans might become a part of the Kingdom of God. So we become a part of the highest kingdom by way of death, but <u>not our death</u>, because the shedding of our blood would not have remitted our sins. <u>Jesus died</u> so that we could become a part of God's kingdom. It is His blood that alone can remit sin. (Hebrews 9:22)

Genesis 1:26-28…The Giver

Genesis 1:26-28 states, "So God said, Let us make man in our image, after our likeness; and let them have dominion over the fish of the sea, and over the fowl of the air, and over the cattle, and over all the earth, and over every creeping thing that creepeth upon the earth. So God created man in his own image, in the image of God created he him; male and female created he them. And God <u>blessed</u> them, and God said unto them, Be fruitful, and multiply, and replenish the earth."

God, being a giver by nature, must have a "receiver" in order to fulfill His need to be a giver. I believe one of the reasons that He created man was so that He would have a receiver of His blessings, because right after He created Adam and Eve He <u>blessed</u> them. I believe that He was full of joy because He now had someone to bless. God is a giver. "For God so loved the world that He gave His only begotten Son..." He gives and gives...and He still gives. He gives because that is His nature. He's a giver! He demonstrated that fact at the very beginning as one of His first acts after He created man was to bless him. He gives, gives, and gives some more.

Genesis 4:1-5...Cain and Abel

I discuss this principle in detail in my book entitled "It's All in the Blood." Genesis 4:1 declares, "And Adam knew Eve his wife; and she conceived, and bare Cain, and said, I have gotten a man from the Lord." As a side note, it was important that Eve understood that she didn't receive a man <u>from</u> Adam. She received a man <u>through</u> Adam but <u>from the Lord!</u> We must understand that when God blesses us with children, they come from Him!

Genesis 4:2:2-5 states, "And she again bare his brother Abel. And Abel was a keeper of sheep, but Cain was a tiller of the ground. And in process of time it came to pass, that Cain brought of the fruit of the ground an offering unto the Lord. And Abel, he also brought of the firstlings of his flock and of the fat thereof. And the Lord had respect unto Abel and to his offering. But unto Cain and to his offering he had not respect. And Cain was very wroth, and his countenance fell."

We have all likely heard, and preached on, the differences in the two offerings which caused God to receive Abel's offering but not Cain's offering. One important difference is that Abel's was a blood offering from something God made, while Cain's offering came from the ground that Cain himself had tilled. Another interesting fact to note is that prior to the events in Genesis 4, God had cursed the ground as a result of the fall (Genesis 3). Therefore, by his offering, *Cain was trying to convince God to accept something He had already cursed*. However, God will not compromise, and what He curses is cursed. Therefore, by offering the fruit of the ground, Cain was asking God to receive something He had already cursed.

Genesis 6:19-21...Food in the Ark

Genesis 6:20-21 contains the account of the animals coming into the ark that Noah built. Verse 19 states, "And of every living thing of all flesh, two of every sort shall thou bring into the ark, to keep them alive with thee; they shall be male and female. Of fowls after their kind, and of cattle after their kind, of every creeping thing of the earth after his kind, two of every sort shall come unto thee, to keep them alive."

As a little boy growing up in church I often wondered how Noah was able to get all of those animals in the ark. I knew enough to know that a man that was well over a hundred years old wasn't quick enough to catch a fox! How then did he get those animals into the ark?

Please note verse 21, which declares, "And take thou unto thee of all food that is eaten, and thou shalt gather it to thee; and it shall be for food for thee, and for them." Noah put the <u>food</u> in the ark first...and animals instinctively go to food. In my mind's eye, I can see Noah having to turn animals away because they were smelling and desiring the food!

We can apply this truth spiritually because many ministers struggle to get people into their pews. I believe it is important that in every gathering, in order to draw people, there must be food (life-changing truth from the Word of God) in the ark (the church or assembly in which we gather). <u>If we have food in the ark, people will come</u>. We won't have to coerce or beg people to come in, because God created people to desire nourishment, both physically and spiritually. People crave food! Noah understood the animals' God-given instinctive need for food and we must understand people's God-given instinctive need for spiritual food and provide it for them!

Genesis 9:20-21...Drunk on Success

Genesis 9:20-21 declares, "And Noah began to be an husbandman, and he planted a vineyard. And he drank of the wine, and was drunken; and he was uncovered within his tent." Noah planted a vineyard, which was successful, and he drank of the fruit of the vine and became drunk. You could say that Noah got drunk on his own success. I have often said that it is just as dangerous to be successful as it is to be a failure. The temptations are the same. When we start believing our "press reports," or when some well-meaning person tells us how great we are, we are in danger of falling. When we start eating or drinking from our own success, trouble is lurking!

Genesis 17:1-15...The Covenant Name

I discuss the ten steps of blood covenant in detail in my book entitled "The Blood Covenant." Please note that God made covenant with Abraham. One of the important steps of entering into blood covenant is the exchange of names. One person takes part of the name of the other, who in turn takes part of the name of the first.

Genesis 17:5 states, "Neither shall thy name any more be called Abram, but thy name shall be Abraham; for a father of many nations have I made thee." Verse 15 declares, "And God said unto Abraham, As for Sarai they wife, thou shalt not call her name Sarai, but Sarah shall her name be."

The meanings of the names themselves are very significant, and even the spelling of the names in English is quite revealing. The name for God is Yah, but the "Y" is silent so therefore we have "ah." If we begin with "Abram" and insert "ah," we arrive at "Abraham." God inserted His name into Abram's as part of the blood covenant!

Likewise, if we start with "Sarai" and remove the "i" (which, incidentally, needs to be done in our selfish nature...removing the "I"), then we add "ah" onto the end, the resulting name is "Sarah." Again, God inserted His name into Sarai's as a sign of blood covenant!

From that time forward, when anyone spoke Abraham or Sarah's name, they were speaking God's name as well, which was a sign to all that Abraham and Sarah were in blood covenant with God!

Genesis 27:21-23...Follow What You Hear, Not What You Feel

Genesis 27:1-46 contains the account of Isaac giving the blessing to his son. Esau was the eldest of twin sons and therefore rightfully deserved the blessing of the firstborn. Esau was a hairy man and his twin brother Jacob was not. Rebekah helped Jacob put goatskins on his arms in an attempt to deceive Isaac into thinking that Jacob was Esau and therefore receive the blessing that was meant for the firstborn son.

Genesis 27:21 declares, "And Isaac said unto Jacob, Come near, I pray thee, that I may feel thee, my son, whether thou be my very son Esau or not." Esau was a very hairy man, and since Isaac's eyesight was failing, he asked for the young man to come near so he could feel his arms to try to confirm his identify as Esau. Genesis 27:22-23 states, "And Jacob went near unto Isaac his father; and he felt him, and said, The voice is Jacob's voice, but the hands are the hands of Esau. And he discerned him not, because his hands were hairy, as his brother Esau's hands: so he blessed him."

Rebekah's plan succeeded. Isaac misidentified Jacob as Esau and therefore mistakenly gave Jacob the blessing that was rightfully Esau's as the firstborn son. *The reason Isaac made the mistake is because he made his decision on the basis of what he felt rather than what he heard.* Jacob heard the voice of Jacob, but felt the arms of "Esau." From this incident, we must learn and apply this key principle in our lives: *We must make our decisions based on what we hear from God rather than what we feel in our natural senses or emotions!*

Genesis 28:11-12...Ascending and Descending

Chapter 28 relates the account when Jacob was on the run because he was fearful that Esau was angry and looking for him. One night, after the sun had set, Genesis 28:11-12 declares

"....he took of the stones of that place, and put them for his pillows, and lay down in that place to sleep. And he dreamed, and behold a ladder set up on the earth, and the top of it reached to heaven; and behold the angels of God ascending and descending on it."

Every word and every phrase, and the ordering of every word, is important in the Bible. Jacob saw the angels "ascending and descending" in that order, and not "descending and ascending." This means that the angels ascended first, and then descended, which teaches us a key truth that the angels were with Jacob all the time.

Also, according to Chapter 2 of John's gospel, Nathaniel was not initially convinced that Jesus was the Messiah, but then Jesus said to him, "I saw you under the fig tree." That was significant because in that culture the houses were very small, and some families would have a fig tree in their yard. Family members would sit under their fig tree to meditate, study the scriptures, and pray. The fig tree essentially created a kind of "outdoor room" that they used for study and meditation. Nathaniel was a "fig tree guy." Jesus saw him before he saw Jesus, and Jesus went on to effectively tell Nathaniel that there were many things he would see in the days ahead that were unlike anything he had ever seen. One of the things that Jesus told Nathaniel he would see were "the angels ascending and descending." Again, this is exactly in the same order as in Jacob's account (Genesis 28:11-12)...ascending then descending, and it reiterates that angels are with us!

I believe we don't wholly appreciate or realize the truth that the angels are with us. We have no idea how often God, through His angels, may have saved us from disaster. We all have to sleep sometimes, but we have angels who never sleep continually watching over us.

It is important for us to know that the angels are always with us. Jacob was in a dark and difficult time of doubt, confusion, and trouble. He wasn't sure if his brother Esau, or even God, was angry with him. Jacob had been a deceiver and had done some bad things. Yet, even in his condition, the angels were with him! Where were the angels? Ascending and descending....ascending to the throne of God and bringing the help of heaven to Jacob in his time of need.

Genesis 35:18-19...We Are Who Our Father Says We Are!

The account of Rachel giving birth to Benjamin is recorded in Genesis 35:18-19, which states, "And it came to pass, as her soul was in departing, (for she died) that she called his name Benoni: but his father called him Benjamin." The baby's mother Rachel named him "Benoni" which means "son of my sorrow," but his father Jacob renamed him Benjamin which means "son of my right hand. The two names are diametrically opposed in meaning. Jacob "overruled" Rachel's name for the baby (son of my sorrow) by naming him Benjamin, thereby declaring that the boy was the son of his right hand, which means the son of his strength. The principle here is that _we are who our Father says we are_.

Before Jesus was born, God the Father sent an angel to both Mary and Joseph to tell them what name they should give to the child. The angel said, "....thou shalt call his name Jesus: for he shall save his people from their sins." (Matthew 1:21) Father was the only one who was really qualified to name Him. Neither Joseph nor Mary was qualified because, though they knew the baby was a gift from God, they didn't know the baby's mission. Father alone knew the baby's mission. Father alone knew He was to be our Savior and our Lord. Mary and Joseph obediently followed the instruction of the angel and named Him Jesus.

Genesis 37:31...The Coat of Many Colors

Genesis 37:31 states, "And they took Joseph's coat, and killed a kid of the goats, and dipped the coat in the blood." The Hebrew word translated "dipped" is a very strong word which means "to soak, to plunge, or to cause to penetrate throughout." It means to cause it to penetrate every fiber. This should encourage us as the Body of Christ because, we are comprised of people of many races and ethnicities, yet our color distinction disappears when we're soaked in the blood. The color of our skin does not matter, because we are all one in Christ and in perfect unity!

Leviticus 16:1-22...The Scapegoat

Leviticus Chapter 16 contains the account of how God had commanded His people to deal with their sin problem via the scapegoat. Leviticus 16:5-10 states, "And he shall take of the congregation of the children of Israel two kids of the goats for a sin offering, and one ram for a burnt offering. And Aaron shall offer his bullock of the sin offering, which is for himself, and make an atonement for himself, and for his house. And he shall take the two goats, and present them before the Lord at the door of the tabernacle of the congregation. And Aaron shall cast lots upon the two goats; one lot for the Lord, and the other lot for the scapegoat. And Aaron shall bring the goat upon which the Lord's lot fell, and offer him for a sin offering. But the goat, on which the lot fell to be the scapegoat, shall be presented alive before the Lord, to make an atonement with him, and to let him go for a scapegoat into the wilderness."

Leviticus 16:20-22 declares, "And when he hath made an end of reconciling the holy place, and the tabernacle of the congregation, and the altar, he shall bring the live goat; And Aaron shall lay both his hands upon the head of the live goat, and confess over him all the iniquities of the children of Israel, and all their transgressions in all their sins, putting them upon the head of the goat, and shall send him away by the hand of a fit man into the wilderness. And the goat shall bear upon him all their iniquities unto a land not inhabited; and he shall let go the goat in the wilderness."

Two steps are important in this process: <u>untie</u> and <u>let go</u>. This was a very important part of dealing with their iniquities, trespasses, and sins. Once Aaron had laid his hands on the scapegoat and effectively transferred the people's sin to the goat in the eyes of God, they then had to <u>untie</u> that goat and send it (<u>let it go</u>) into the wilderness. If they didn't untie it, they would have a constant reminder of their sins which they would have to look upon over and over. A big part of moving on and remembering our sins no more is untying the scapegoat. Many people still have their goat tied right beside them. That goat must go! When the Hebrews sent the goat off into the wilderness they never saw him again and did not think about him any longer.

As recorded in Jeremiah 31:34, God declares that He remembers our sins no more. I've heard people say "God forgives and forgets," but that's technically not true. The Bible does not say that God forgives and forgets. The word "forgets" suggests a loss of control, and God <u>never</u> loses control since He is omniscient (all-knowing). He knows everything and cannot forget. He simply chooses "not to remember." He looks at us in love and chooses not to think about the sin for which we have repented. However, we tend to beat ourselves up about our past sins rather than doing as God does, choosing not to dwell on them or remember them.

Get rid of your goat, because the goat cannot minister to you or bring you life. Repent of your sins and leave them at the foot of the cross. Make the conscious choice not to remember those sins any longer!

Numbers 21:8-9...Motives and Worship

Numbers 21:8-9 declares, "And the Lord said unto Moses, Make thee a fiery serpent, and set it upon a pole; and it shall come to pass, that every one that is bitten, when he looketh upon it, shall live. And Moses made a serpent of brass, and put it upon a pole, and it came to pass, that if a serpent had bitten any man, when he beheld the serpent of brass, he lived."

II Kings 18:4 gives the account of King Hezekiah "cleaning up" when he came to reign. Please note that this is <u>seven hundred years</u> after the fiery serpent was erected. "He removed the high places, and brake the images, and cut down the groves, and brake in pieces the brazen serpent that Moses had made; for unto those days the children of Israel did burn incense to it; and he called it Nehushtan."

Over seven hundred years later, they were worshipping the <u>instrument</u> through which God brought the blessing rather than worshipping the <u>God</u> of the blessing. They made an idol out of the instrument and I believe our human tendency is to do the very same thing! I have observed that many of the things that we have done in the kingdoms of the world, we have carried as baggage into the Kingdom of God. For example, we have our own role models, superstars and heroes in the church world. I certainly believe that it is scriptural to honor those to whom honor is due, but we must be careful to keep our focus on God.

The lesson of the brazen serpent is that it is dangerous when we base our future on that which God used in the past. Hezekiah effectively said, "We're not getting anywhere, we're not going on, and we won't have freedom until we knock that old image down because that serpent on a pole is nothing without God." It's God's touch that gives the instrument its value. May God ever keep us humble in our relationships to one another. Without God's touch there is nothing good in our humanity. Flesh is flesh. Jesus said something in the wilderness of temptation which is significant in this regard. Matthew 4:10 declares, "Then saith Jesus unto him," that is unto Satan, "Get thee hence, Satan; for it is written," (quoting Deuteronomy 6:13) "Thou shalt worship the Lord thy God, and him only shalt thou serve."

Notice the conjunction *and* that ties the thought of worship in with the thought of service. *I firmly believe that the only kind of service that is acceptable to God and has eternal significance is to serve out of the motive of worship.* There are motives of all kinds. Some people serve out of obligation, and they can therefore become disgruntled, weary. Some serve out of a desire for visibility, to be seen or recognized, and if they don't receive the recognition or adulation they expect, they become disappointed or feel unappreciated. If our motives aren't pure, when times get tough, we will surely become frustrated.

Everyone, regardless of the church or ministry in which they serve, will be faced with difficulty and unpleasantness in the course of their service to God. These things can certainly drain a pastor. Sometimes pastors spend more time with the leaders than the "leadees." If we can get people to serve simply as an act of worship to God, they won't need to constantly be "petted and patted."

I recall a time I was on a prolonged fast when I awoke not feeling very well one morning. I was weary, hungry, and weak. I seemingly bumped into every wall between my bedroom and the bathroom, and I heard this coming out of my mouth, "Jesus, I would only do this for you." There is no other reward. I always felt as a pastor if people serve as an act of worship they would never be disappointed, because God inevitably rewards, not only temporally but also eternally, those whose motives are pure.

To use a sports analogy, we must "play to the throne rather than the grandstand." At any sports contest, regardless of how skilled the athlete may be or how well he is performing, there will inevitably be a number of spectators booing him. Athletes train themselves to tune out that negativity and focus on their task at hand. We must do the same thing in God's kingdom. If we are not listening for the cheers, we won't hear the boos. The boos are almost always going to be there. The best way to tune out the boos is for each of us to play to the throne. We should be performing for an audience of one. The only opinion that should matter to us is God's opinion!

Hebrews 12:1 states, "Wherefore seeing we also are compassed about with so great a cloud of witnesses, let us lay aside every weight, and the sin which doth so easily beset us." There will always be a grandstand, but that shouldn't be our motivation. Let's serve as an act of worship.

Ruth 1:14...Kisser or Cleaver?

The difference between the hearts of Orpah and Ruth was revealed by the manner in which they reacted to their mother-in-law Naomi's impending departure. Ruth 1:14 states, "And they lifted up their voice, and wept again: and Orpah kissed her mother-in-law; but Ruth clave unto her." Please note that Orpah <u>kissed</u> Naomi but Ruth <u>clave</u> unto her. The word "clave" (or "cleaved") means "to be joined, to be fastened to." Kissing is an external show of affection but doesn't necessarily reflect a deep commitment. Judas was a kisser, but he wasn't a cleaver. There is a difference between people deciding to believe in Jesus and committing to follow Him. The end purpose of God is not only to have people believe in Him, but for them also to commit to follow Him.

I Samuel 10:1...Anointed by Man or God?

Saul was anointed with a <u>vial</u> of oil according to I Samuel 10:1, and David was anointed with a <u>horn</u> of oil, according to I

Samuel 16:13. A vial is man-made but a ram's horn is something that God made. There is a difference between being anointed by man and being anointed by God. That difference is evident in the contrasting lives of Saul and David.

I Samuel 17:26-46...Focus on God, Not the Giant

The account of David representing Israel against the Philistine giant Goliath is found in I Samuel 17:26-46. David referred to Goliath five times in that account. Two times (verses 26 and 37), David called him "this Philistine." Twice (verses 26 and 36), he referred to him as "this uncircumcised Philistine," and in verse 46 he called him "the host of the Philistines." It is interesting that David did not call him a giant even once. Others referred to Goliath as a giant, but David did not. He knew that God was bigger than Goliath and all of the "giants" of this world.

Numbers 13:1-33 contains the account of the twelve Hebrew spies reporting to Moses what they had observed in Canaan. Note that, just as David would do many years later in his encounter with Goliath, Joshua and Caleb chose to focus on the faithfulness of God and not on the giants. Numbers 13:30 states, "And Caleb stilled the people before Moses, and said, Let us go up at once, and possess it; for we are well able to overcome it." Joshua and Caleb did not focus on the giants, but rather on God's power and promise. However, the other spies saw things differently according to their report recorded in Numbers 13:33, which declares, "And there we saw the giants, the sons of Anak, which come of the giants: and we were in our own sight as grasshoppers, and so we were in their sight."

The lesson? We must focus on God and His promises to us rather than the giants. We are not "grasshoppers" when God is working in us and through us. We don't see ourselves as a grasshopper unless we see our enemy as a giant.

II Samuel 6:16...Looking Through a Window

David's wife Michal had great difficulty with David's celebratory dance in response to the return of the Ark of the Covenant (the presence of God) to the people of God. II Samuel 6:16 states that Michal was looking through her window as she was watching David dance. God was doing something great all around her, but not only did she refuse to participate in the joyful celebration, but she expressed her disdain for it. It is interesting that she was observing what God was doing through her "window." Windows have limitations not only in size but also in clarity. When we are looking through "windows," we can be limited as to what we see when God is moving. There are things such as traditions, biases, religious practices, and dogma which can, like a window, affect our view of what God is doing or which can, like a prism, cause us to see a distorted picture of what God is doing.

Michal's problem was that she wasn't <u>involved</u> in what God was doing...instead, she was looking at it from a distance with a restricted view. She was a spectator rather than a participant, and I have learned that spectators can be unfairly critical of participants. It is easy to sit idly by and criticize rather than make the sacrifice, and put forth the effort, to get involved. A "window spectator" can easily become cynical and negative, but a participant enjoys the satisfaction of being involved and committed. Michal was bitter and angry, but David was full of the joy of the Lord because he was in His presence! (Psalm 16:11)

II Samuel 24:24...There is a Cost

Araunah the Jebusite offered to give his threshing floor, at no cost, to David so he could establish an altar of worship to God there, but David responded, "....I will surely buy it of thee at a price; neither will I offer burnt offerings unto the Lord my God of that which doth cost me nothing."

I believe that anyone that has served the Lord understands that there is a cost associated with being in ministry. I have heard it said, in reference to fulltime ministry, "If you can do anything else and be happy, do it, but if you can't, then you've been called." There is a cost to being a minister. I can go to the store and buy a bottle of olive oil for ten dollars, but if I really want to know the true cost of the olive oil, I shouldn't ask the cashier, I should ask the olive! The cost of the olive oil to me is ten dollars, but it cost the olive its life. Similarly, there is a cost associated with giving our lives in ministry and service to the Lord.

II Kings 4:2...Never Without Oil

II Kings 4:2 contains the account of a widow who only had one pot of oil. The word "pot" in the Hebrew is *acuwk* and the word means "the anointing." I think of Jesus, at the completion of His earthly ministry, ascending to Heaven after assuring the disciples that they would not be left comfortless. Jesus said, "I will send you a comforter." He was essentially saying, "I will not leave your house empty. I will send you the oil so that you have a pot of oil and you will never be without!" We, as the church, are not without the presence and the power of the Holy Spirit. We need to understand the importance, value, and significance of that truth, because the anointing of the Holy Spirit is our lifeline to accomplishing and fulfilling everything that our Father has given us to do.

II Kings 6:1-7...The Cutting Edge

The account of the sons of the prophets building a larger dwelling is found in II Kings 6:1-7. While working, one of the men lost the head of the axe he was using. He was troubled not only by the fact he lost the axe head, but also by the fact that the axe was borrowed. He effectively lost the sharpness, the keenness, the cutting edge he had, while he was involved in the work of the Lord. He was doing what he ought to be doing, but he had lost the cutting edge.

What a cry there should be in every one of our hearts to make certain this doesn't happen to us. I have experienced times in my life when I felt like I was missing something in my ministry and I had lost the sharpness, the cutting edge. Those are the times we need to get on our faces before the Lord and ask Him to help us find it again, because if we keep on swinging without the cutting edge, we are going to bruise the tree.

II Chronicles 24:14...The Purpose of the Vessels

The account of finishing the house of the Lord is recorded in II Chronicles 24:14 which states, "And when they had finished it, they brought the rest of the money before the king and Jehoiada, whereof were made vessels for the house of the Lord, even vessels to minister, and to offer withal, and spoons, and vessels of gold and silver. Any they offered burnt offerings in the house of the lord continually all the days of Jehoiada."

Note that these vessels had two purposes in the house of the Lord - to minister and to offer. The Hebrew word translated "minister" is *shareth*, which means "service; to serve." The Hebrew word translated "offer" is *alah*, which means "to cause to go up." Each of us, as a vessel in the house of the Lord, has these same two purposes. One purpose is to <u>minister</u>, which is horizontal service to one another, and the other is to <u>offer up</u>, which is to vertical ministry unto the Lord. In the church, we must avoid the predominant attitude of the world, which is that of being a consumer. We must understand that we receive in order to give. We are blessed in order to be a blessing and fulfill our purpose in God's house. When we come to church gatherings, we have the privilege of ministering to Him (offering up praise) and to serve others as a functional vessel in the house of the Lord. It involves both the vertical and the horizontal.

Song of Solomon 6:1...Keeping Our Own Vineyard

Song of Solomon 6:1 declares, "Look not upon me, because I am black, because the sun hath looked upon me; my mother's children were angry with me; they made me the keeper of the vineyards; but mine own vineyard have I not kept."

There is a principle found in this verse which is significant to everyone that has a responsibility in any area of leadership in God's kingdom. *We must keep our own vineyard.* When we are given a responsibility in the house of the Lord, it is never to replace or reduce the importance of our relationship to the Lord. We must never trade relationship for responsibility, or we will lose both.

I recall, as a young man playing athletics, how we worked all season to get in the playoffs, yet the coaches' message was consistent whether it was a regular season game or a playoff game. Some would ask, "What are we going to do coach? Have you devised a new secret plan for victory? Have you come up with a new strategy to get the job done and win the game?" The coach would inevitably say, "No, we are going to do the very same things that got us here." The lesson for us is that once we are placed in a position of responsibility, we should never depart from doing the things that brought us the responsibility, especially maintaining a vibrant, healthy relationship with God and others. Relationship is vital, and in fact we need relationship more than ever when we carry more responsibility.

Song of Solomon 1:9...Pulling the King's Chariots

Song of Solomon 1:9 declares, "I have compared thee, O my love, to a company of horses in Pharaoh's chariots." This particular analogy is important because there was nothing considered as honorable or valuable as the horses that pulled Pharaoh's chariots. These horses were hand-picked based on certain criteria, and this is significant because, in type, we are the horses pulling the King's chariot. Pharaoh wouldn't accept just any horse. Each horse had to pass through a three stage process to be fit for Pharaoh's service, to pull his chariots.

The first step in the process was the <u>blood</u> test. The horse was chosen on the basis of the blood. Pharaoh sent out people, called mediators, to search for his horses. There was no restriction placed on the horse's cost or from how far away the horse could be purchased. Those things didn't matter to Pharaoh. The mediators had one important characteristic - they knew the heart of the king. They knew the things that would please Pharaoh and nothing less was acceptable, so they went about their task on that basis. They didn't choose just any horse. The horses were chosen on the basis of the blood, that is, the horses were judged by who their father was, their grandfather, and their great-grandfather. They would look back as far as six or seven generations. The mediators didn't look at the color of the horse's hair or the size of the horse. They looked at the horse's heritage. In order to choose him, the mediator's wanted to know who his father is!

The second step was that the horses had to be <u>bought</u>. They weren't donated or traded. They had to be purchased, and there was no price that was too high as far as Pharaoh was concerned. He effectively said, "I will pay anything because that's how valuable you are to me." We know that our Lord did exactly the same thing when He paid the supreme price for us.

The third step was that, once a horse passed the blood test and was purchased for a price, he had to be <u>broken</u>. The hoses were of no use to the Pharaoh unless they responded to his voice. When they were in the midst of the noise and confusion of the battlefield, they had to ignore every other noise and distraction and be finely tuned only to the voice of their Pharaoh, so that when he gave direction, they would respond.

Song of Solomon 2:9...Like the Hart

Song of Solomon 2:9 states, "My beloved is like a roe or a young hart; behold he standeth behind our wall, he looketh forth at the windows, shewing himself through the lattice."

In His Word, God gives us many pictures and analogies, and if we study and search out the truth, we can come to a clearer understanding of what He is looking for from our lives. Song of Solomon 2:9 refers to a hart, which is a deer. There were three species of deer in Palestine in Bible times, and the most predominant species is the one referred to in the Bible about twenty-one times, called a red deer. This deer was about the same size as a modern white-tailed deer. Once the male red deer reached five years of age, he was called a hart. The female, once she reached three years of age, was called a hind.

The hart had several interesting characteristics. One is that the hart is born with an instinct that his enemy is the serpent. He hates the serpent from the moment he's born. My mind goes back to Genesis 3:15, where God said; "...and I will put enmity between thee and the woman, and between thy seed and her seed." The hart carries a natural enmity for the serpent.

The second thing that is interesting is that the hart knows by instinct where serpents hide. I'm reminded of what the apostle Paul, when speaking of the devil, said when he said we are not ignorant of his devices. (II Corinthians 2:11) The hart knows instinctively that serpents hide in holes.

A third thing about the hart is that when he wants to drive a serpent out of a hole, he breathes down the hole. The serpent can't stand the breath of a hart, so he comes slithering out. We have in us the breath of God, the Holy Spirit. The Apostle Paul wrote to the Colossian church (Colossians 2:15) that Jesus spoiled principalities, making a shew of them openly. Jesus drove the demonic forces "out of their hole" and exposed them for all to see.

After the hart drives the serpent out of the hole, he will grab it, kill it, and devour it. After the hart devours the serpent, there is an intense thirst that comes to the hart, so intense that he must have water. Psalm 42:1 declares, "As the hart panteth after the water brooks, so panteth my soul after thee oh God." It is interesting to note that as Jesus was devouring the serpent (Satan) on the cross, He said, "I thirst!"

The enmity between the hart and the serpent continues even after the hart dies. Even today, if a man is traveling in an area that is infested with serpents, if he covers himself at night with hart skin, the serpent won't touch him. The devil won't have any part of Jesus because he knows that he has already been conquered.

The final thing of note is that the only antidote to the venom of the serpent is the blood of the hart. When bitten by a serpent, run to the blood! Revelation 12:12 declares, "And they overcame him by the blood of the Lamb, and by the word of their testimony." We need to emphasize the blood more this day and hour. There is power in the blood.

Isaiah 10:27…Breaking vs. Destroying the Yoke

Isaiah 10:27 declares, "….the yoke shall be destroyed because of the anointing" and Isaiah 58:6 states, "Is not this the fast that I have chosen?....that ye break every yoke?" Please note that there is a difference between *breaking* the yoke and *destroying* the yoke, and there is a different Hebrew word used for each of these actions. The Hebrew word *nathaq* is translated to break the yoke and it means "to tear off or to break off." The Hebrew word *chabal* is found in Isaiah 10:27 and it means "destroyed without the benefit of ever reappearing; dealt with in finality." Both words are important and they both have their place. Fasting has its place and many of its advantages are listed in Isaiah Chapter 58. Fasting can <u>break</u> the yoke, but it is only the anointing that can <u>destroy</u> the yoke.

Isaiah 40:2...Giving the Double

Isaiah 40:2 declares, "Speak ye comfortably to Jerusalem, and cry unto her, that her warfare is accomplished, that her iniquity is pardoned; for she hath received of the Lord's hand double for all her sins."

This verse speaks of the Lord giving His people "double" in pardoning their sins. It can be a puzzling verse unless we understand a custom called "giving the double" which was practiced in Bible times regarding the elimination of a debt. When someone found themselves in a situation in which they were so indebted that they had reached a point of near hopelessness, there was a practice they could follow in the hope that their debts could be forgiven.

The debtor would take a goat skin and on it write a list of all of his creditors and the amount owed to each. He then had to nail the goat skin to the outside of the front door of his house. This list was effectively an open declaration that he had failed and that he could not resolve his debt, and it was also an announcement to everyone that walked by on the street that there is real trouble in the house. If any of the creditors walked by and saw his name and debt amount on the list, he had the option of going up to the goat skin and drawing a line through that item, effectively declaring, "I cancel that part of your debt and you can forget about paying that." However, if there was a man of means who had the resources to pay off all of the debt, he could take the bottom of the goat skin, roll it up over the top and drive a nail through it such that the debts could no longer be seen. This was called "giving the double." The debt was entirely canceled and no one could even see what the debt had been.

Hundreds of years after Isaiah 40 was written, there were nails driven into Jesus' hands and feet on the cross. Jesus died so that our sin-debt would be paid in full. Jesus "gave the double." The words of a beautiful hymn declare, "Jesus paid it all, all to Him I owe, sin has left a crimson stain, He washed it white as snow." His mercy and grace paid our debt and washed our sins away. Jesus walked down our street one day, saw our goat skin, and canceled our debt by being nailed to the cross. He gave the double!

Isaiah 43:2..."When" and "Through"

Isaiah 43:2 states, "When thou passest through the waters, I will be with thee; and through the rivers, they shall not overflow thee; when thou walkest through the fire, thou shalt not be burned; neither shall the flame kindle upon thee." There are two words that are key to me in this verse - <u>when</u> and <u>through</u>.

In all three cases, when referring to the trials of water, rivers, and fire, the word "if" is not used, but the word "when." This means that trouble and trials are inevitable for all of us. It is not a matter of "if" we will face challenges, but "when!" Please also note John 16:33 in this regard.

The second word that is important is the word "through." Please note that the word "into" isn't used. By definition, the word "through" implies that you are going to come out the other end. We must remember that God will bring us "through" the trials we face. We will not perish in them!

Jeremiah 12:5...It's Harvest Time

Jeremiah 12:5 declares, "If thou hast run with the footmen, and they have wearied thee, then how canst thou contend with horses? And if in the land of peace, wherein thou trustedst, they wearied thee, then how wilt thou do in the swelling of Jordan?"

The phrase "the swelling of Jordan" is significant in this verse. Joshua 3:15 states, "....for Jordan overfloweth all his banks all the time of harvest." The Jordan River swells and overflows during the harvest, which means that Jeremiah 12:5 is referring to the time of the harvest. I believe one of the things God is saying to the church today is "Get strong and get tough, get rid of all whining and complaining. It is harvest time!" As the harvest continues to build and we continue to bring more people into God's kingdom, there will be an increasing level of opposition by the enemy such as we have never seen before. God is saying,

"Get tough, get strong, get your armor on, and get ready because we're going to win, but it won't be without overcoming."

We must be ready to run. I don't know what the future holds, but my confidence is neither in a political party nor in any man. My confidence is in the Lord and the thing that's important to me is that it's harvest time.

Jeremiah 18:1-2...Knowing What He Means

Jeremiah 18:1-2 declares, "The word which came to Jeremiah from the Lord, saying, Arise and go down to the potter's house, and there I will cause thee to hear my words." The Hebrew word translated "hear" is *shama,* which means "to discern or understand," and the word translated "words" is the Hebrew word *dabar,* which means "what I am saying." God was instructing Jeremiah to go to the potter's house so he could not only hear God's voice, but so he could also understand what God meant by what He was saying.

I believe there is a difference between understanding what God means by what He says as opposed to simply recognizing His voice. Jesus said in John 10:4 "My sheep know my voice and the voice of another they will not follow." I believe <u>recognizing</u> His voice is a birthright of Christians, but <u>understanding</u> what He means is a mark of maturity.

In the natural world, a baby instinctively knows the voice of his or her mother. When my children were young, I would baby-sit when my wife wasn't home. On one occasion, one of my infant sons would not be quiet and I could not calm him down no matter how hard I tried. After what seemed like an eternity, my wife came through the door and said, "What's the matter honey?" and my son instantly calmed down. He knew the sound of his mother's voice. In John 10:10, Jesus was effectively saying that He gave His sheep a birthright to hear and recognize His voice. When we are born-again we have a birth-right to <u>recognize</u> His voice, but it takes a trip to the potter's house to know what He <u>means</u> by what He says. I want to understand what He means by what He says!

Ezekiel 3:1-3...Delivering the Word with the Right Spirit

Ezekiel received the following instruction from God, as recorded in Ezekiel 3:1, which states, "Moreover he said unto me, Son of man, eat that thou findest; eat this roll and go speak unto the house of Israel." Verse 3 declares, "And he said unto me, Son of man, cause thy belly to eat, and fill thy bowels with this roll (with this word) that I give thee. Then did I eat it; and it was in my mouth as honey for sweetness."

Ezekiel had the word and the commission, but he didn't yet have the release to preach the word he was given. He didn't receive the release until he sat where the people sit. Ezekiel 3:12-14 states, "Then the spirit took me up, and I heard behind me a voice of a great rushing, saying, Blessed be the glory of the Lord from his place. I heard also the noise of the wings of the living creatures that touched one another, and the noise of the wheels over against them, and a noise of a great rushing. So the spirit lifted me up, and took me away, and I went in bitterness, in the heat of my spirit; but the hand of the Lord was strong upon me."

God still had to do something in him so that he didn't minister in anger or bitterness.

Verse 15 declares, "Then I came to them of the captivity at Telabib, that dwell by the river of Chebar, and I sat where they sat, and remained there astonished among them seven days." Seven is the number of completion. Verses 16 and 17 state, "And it came to pass at the end of seven days, that the word of the Lord came unto me, saying, Son of man, I have made thee a watchman unto the house of Israel; therefore hear the word at my mouth, and give them warning from me."

I see in this passage a need to not only <u>have</u> the Word, but to be ready to <u>deliver</u> the Word. Those of us who have been in ministry for any length of time know that delivering the Word clearly is absolutely essential. We can have the Word but if the Spirit isn't there to help us deliver it, we can miss God's purpose. Ezekiel had the Word, but he had bitterness and anger in his spirit. Perhaps he was thinking, "How could these people get themselves into such a mess?" God effectively said, "Settle down, you have the Word but now I'm going to give you the right spirit. Go sit where they sit." God didn't tell Ezekiel to become one of them but He told him to sit where they sit. I have a Native American background, and one of the phrases I've heard often is, "Don't judge a man until you've walked a mile in his moccasins."

Ezekiel had to go through preparation in order to effectively carry out the task, the call, which had been placed upon him. It's easy to simply get angry, but God doesn't want us to deliver His Word when our spirit isn't right. If we submit ourselves to God, He will prepare us to properly deliver His Word, and give us the capacity to do so with love and power.

Daniel 3 and Daniel 6...Delivered In the Trial, Not From It

Chapter 3 of the Book of Daniel contains the account of the three Hebrew children (Shadrach, Meshach, and Abednego) being thrown into the fiery furnace by King Nebuchadnezzar because they refused to worship idols. God miraculously kept them from perishing in the flames, and they emerged from the furnace alive and well, much to Nebuchadnezzar's disbelief! In fact, Daniel 3:27 describes them this way, "....upon whose bodies the fire had no power, nor was an hair of their head singed, neither were their coats changed, nor the smell of fire had passed on them." It's not enough to come out alive. We've got to come out without smelling like smoke!

It is important to note that the three Hebrew children were not delivered <u>from</u> the fiery furnace; they were delivered from the fire while <u>in</u> the furnace. That is not just a play on words. That is what turned the heart of King Nebuchadnezzar. God could have prevented them from entering the furnace, but if that had happened, I believe that Nebuchadnezzar would not have been so deeply affected. Because they endured the furnace and came out without even smelling like smoke, King Nebuchadnezzar turned to God.

Likewise, Daniel wasn't delivered <u>from</u> the lions' den, he was delivered from the mouth of the lions while he was <u>in</u> the den, and that is what changed the heart of King Darius. (Daniel 6:16-24)

Joel 2:28-32…We Need Everyone!

This is the scripture that Peter referenced on the day of Pentecost. Joel 2:28-29 declares, "And it shall come to pass afterward, that I will pour out my spirit upon all flesh; and your sons and your daughters shall prophesy, your old men shall dream dreams, your young men shall see visions; And also upon the servants and upon the handmaids in those days will I pour out my spirit."

In prophesying how God was going to accomplish His purpose and fulfill His promise in the last days through His people, the prophet Joel carefully identified three generations. He identified sons and daughters, old men, and young men. I believe that in the church we must understand that each person and each generation has something to contribute to the whole. The old must learn to embrace the young and the young to embrace the old. Sometimes the young have the attitude that the old are outdated, but they are not any more outdated than the Old Testament is. The Old Testament means the "former" testament, so the older generation is simply the former group. From the young comes energy and vision, and from the old comes experience and wisdom. Putting all of that together produces a dynamic team! There is a reason that God keeps some of the older people around and anoints some of the younger people.

We must learn to appreciate one another and our differences, and draw together knowing that as a unified, anointed company of believers, we can bring in the harvest. The Lord of the harvest has chosen to do it this way. One way to look at Joel 2:28 is to see that God is not leaving anybody out. We have an obligation to reach out to those that may not see everything the way we see it, and may not like everything the way we like it. We need everyone in order to fulfill God's purposes!

Haggai 2:18-19...The Power in the Seed

Haggai 2:18-19 states, "Consider now from this day and upward, from the four and twentieth day of the ninth month, even from the day that the foundation of the Lord's temple was laid, consider it. Is the seed yet in the barn?"

Seeds have the potential of producing something greater and more meaningful than themselves. I remember the first time I went to the store as a child and bought a packet of flower seeds because of the photo on the packet. I didn't have any idea how to grow flowers and perhaps not even the patience to do so. However, the photo on the seed packet is prophetic, because it is a promise that if you allow the seed to do its work, it will produce something greater than itself. The seeds themselves aren't very exciting to look at, but the flowers certainly are! In His teaching, Jesus used seed as a "type" of two things. In one case He used it as a type of the Word of God and in another case He used it as a type of people.

God deposits the Word of God in us, and He also puts things in us such as talents, skills, abilities and anointing. That deposit, that seed, has the potential of bringing out something much greater than what initially appears.

An important characteristic of seeds is that they are born with a destiny to die. Jesus said, as recorded in John 12:24, "....Except a corn of wheat fall into the ground and die, it abideth alone." Unless the seed falls into the ground and goes through the death process, it will never produce everything that it is designed to produce.

Another characteristic of seeds is that in order to fulfill their purpose, they must be sown (planted). When they are planted, they will, by their very nature, bring forth fruit. Conversely, if seed is stored rather than sown it will rot and produce a foul, putrid odor. People can become critical, cynical, and hateful when they try to store what ought to be sown. God said, "Is the seed still in the barn?" We must sow the seed that God has placed in us, and not store it away!

Zechariah 13:1...A Fountain Opened

The powerful, prophetic word of Zechariah 13:1 declares, "In that day there shall be a fountain opened to the house of David and to the inhabitants of Jerusalem for sin and for uncleanness."

The word translated "open" is *pathach* in the Hebrew, which means "let loose or released." The word translated "fountain" is *maqor* in the Hebrew, which means "a container of blood or water." The prophet is saying in that day a container of blood or water will be opened, let loose, and released for uncleanness.

Zechariah 12:10 provides more details on how this fountain will be opened, "And I will pour upon the house of David, and upon the inhabitants of Jerusalem, the spirit of grace and of supplications; and they shall look upon me whom they have pierced, and they shall mourn for him, as one mourneth for his only son, and shall be in bitterness for him, as one that is in bitterness for his firstborn."

I believe the fulfillment of this prophetic word is that the Spirit of grace has let loose and released a container of blood - our Lord Jesus Christ. Jesus is the container, the only one that has ever been clothed in flesh that had pure, uncontaminated blood in His veins.

The Spirit of grace opened the fountain five places:
1) in Jesus' head with the crown of thorns for protection of our thought life,
2) in His back with the stripes for the healing of our bodies,
3) in His hands with the nails so we can use our hands in dedicated service to the Lord,
4) in His feet with the nails so we can walk in the paths of His purpose, and
5) in His side with the sword so we can minister in love and compassion.

I'm so thankful that Jesus wasn't just a fountain *contained*, but rather a fountain *opened*. He freely gave His pure blood that brought cleansing from the impurity of sin, as it says in Zechariah 13:1, "for uncleanness." The only one that can cleanse us and make us free is our Lord Jesus Christ. He was pierced and opened by the Spirit of grace, and the blood that flowed was powerful.

Malachi 4:6 and Revelation 22:21...Curse vs. Grace

The Book of Malachi is the last book of the Old Testament, and the Book of Revelation is the last book of the New Testament. The very last word of the very last verse of Malachi 4:6 is the word "curse." *Please realize that if Jesus hadn't come, that would have been the end of the Bible and the last word of the Bible would have been the word "curse!"*

The last verse of the Book of Revelation (Revelation 22:21) declares "May the grace of the Lord Jesus Christ be with you. Amen." Please note the word <u>grace</u> in the last verse of the Bible! Please note the stark contrast between the way the Old Testament ends and the way the New Testament ends. I am so thankful that the Bible didn't end with Malachi...and the word "curse." I'm so thankful for the New Testament which proclaims to us that God's grace, through Jesus, overcame the curse! We are here today, and we can worship and bless the name of the Lord because we are products of the <u>grace</u> of God and the <u>curse</u> has been forever removed!

Matthew 10:5-14...Handling Rejection

Matthew 10:5-14 records the account of Jesus commissioning His disciples and effectively making them apostles, which means "sent ones." As He was commissioning them and sending them out, He commanded them by saying, "Go not into the way of the

Gentiles, and into any city of the Samaritans enter ye not; But go rather to the lost sheep of the house of Israel. And as ye go, preach, saying, The kingdom of heaven is at hand. Heal the sick, cleanse the lepers, raise the dead, cast out devils, freely ye have received, freely give. Provide neither gold, nor silver, nor brass in your purses. Nor scrip for your journey, neither two coats, neither shoes, nor yet staves; for the workman is worthy of his meat. And into whatsoever city or town ye shall enter, enquire who in it is worthy; and there abide till ye go thence. And when ye come into an house, salute it. And if the house be worthy, let your peace come upon it; but if it be not worthy, let your peace return to you. And whosoever shall not receive you, nor hear your words, when ye depart out of that house or city, shake off the dust of your feet."

When Jesus told them to shake the dust off of their feet, He was effectively saying that He will handle all issues regarding judgment. We aren't called to be amateur judges or juries. God can handle it! Jesus said that it is important that, when rejected, we should "shake off the dust" from our feet. In other words, we cannot carry the rejection to the next house, because we must be prepared to bring peace to the next person we encounter. If we have the dust of rejection all over our feet, we won't be effective in ministering peace to the next house. Being rejected is a part of ministry and of life. One of the subtle strategies of the enemy is to cause rejection to fill our hearts and minds to the point we can no longer be ambassadors of peace. There is something about our flesh, our humanity, that doesn't embrace rejection very well. Therefore, Jesus said it's important that we shake it off. That is the only way we can guarantee our effectiveness. Jesus told the apostles that He was anointing them, giving them authority, commissioning them, and sending them forth. They had everything they would need, but there's one thing they had to learn to do...wipe their feet!

Matthew 13:44...It's OK to Teach It Again!

On several occasions, Jesus was teaching principles of the Kingdom of God and He used the word "Again." It is encouraging to me, and I believe to all ministers, that Jesus used the word "Again" and also the phrase "Again I say unto you" as an introduction when teaching or speaking to His listeners. When I was relatively young in the ministry, I felt that I had to say something unique every time I preached or taught. However, that mentality can be dangerous, because in our eagerness to ever find something new or unique, we can tend to "find" things in the Word that aren't really there, or interpret what we read in the Word in a way that God never meant or intended. It's perfectly fine to re-preach something that God has laid on our hearts, because Jesus Himself preached messages that He had preached before! He said, "And again I say unto you...."

Matthew 13:44...Buying the Whole Field

"Again, the kingdom of heaven is like unto treasure hid in a field; the which when a man hath found, he hideth, and for joy thereof goeth and selleth all that he hath, and buyeth that field." It was the treasure that the man wanted, but in order to obtain the treasure, he had to buy the field. This is a kingdom principle. A field may not only contain the treasure, but also rocks and weeds and other less desirable items that the buyer may not necessarily want to own. We must "buy the field," which means commit ourselves 100%, when we follow Christ. The man sold all he had, signifying total commitment, and bought the entire field.

Let me use an example to illustrate this principle. Over the years, I have officiated at the marriage ceremonies of many couples. One of the things I have always enjoyed is being close enough to the bride and groom to be able to watch their eyes. During the ceremony they are focused only on the treasure. I performed one wedding where I could see that the groom couldn't wait to kiss the bride. When the time finally came, he bent her back to kiss her and the end of her veil swung into the unity candle and caught on fire. The bride was on fire, the groom was having a great time, and I was trying to extinguish the flame with the only thing I had in my hand, my eyeglasses case. It was quite a scene! I always tried to counsel couples before they married that they were "buying the field" when they committed to each other in marriage. They weren't just getting the treasure (their new spouse), but they were "buying" the in-laws (or the outlaws, depending on one's outlook), and everything else, good and bad, that comes along with promising to join together with someone for the rest of their lives.

Likewise, when some people come to Jesus, all they want to do is spend time with Him, but they fail to realize that because they are part of God's family, God's other children are part of the deal! They may only want Jesus, but they must accept His family also, because the family is part of the field.

When we study the Bible, we encounter many scriptures that I call "hallelujah scriptures." These are the scriptures that bless us when we read them and we want to shout "Hallelujah!" However, we also encounter verses that challenge us, or are a little more difficult over which to rejoice, and we may wonder, "Can't I only stick to the hallelujah scriptures?" No! We are to live by <u>every</u> word of God! We must realize that in addition to the promises, there are commandments, correction, and instruction. We buy the field, not just the "treasure!"

Matthew 17:24-27…We Don't Have To, But We Will

Peter asked Jesus about paying taxes. After Jesus said that they really had no obligation to do so, He said, as recorded in Matthew 17:27, "Notwithstanding, lest we should offend them, go thou to the sea, and cast an hook, and take up the fish that first cometh up; and when thou hast opened his mouth, thou shalt find a piece of money; that take, and give unto them for me and thee."

Isn't that a beautiful basis by which to function? "We don't have to, but we're going to…" Jesus was effectively saying, "I don't want to offend them or create a spiritual roadblock in their lives, so we're going to go ahead and pay the tax."

In the Sea of Galilee, there is a fish of the Tilapia species which is referred to as "Saint Peter's fish" because it ties into this particular scripture. In the Hebrew language, the fish's name is Amon, and this fish has a unique characteristic in that the female carries her young offspring in her mouth. She is referred to as "a mouth breeder," and in order to stretch her mouth to prepare her for carrying her young, she actually fills her cheeks with objects from the lake bottom such as stones. When her babies are born, she spits out the stones and then carries and protects her offspring in a cavity in her mouth until they are old enough to be independent and protect themselves. She hides them in the pouch and protects them for the season. God likely used this type of fish, which was perfectly designed to carry items in its mouth, to carry and deliver the coin to Peter to pay the tax. What a sovereign God we serve!

It is always interesting to learn the customs and facts around which these scriptures are written. It gives us a greater appreciation for the sovereignty of God in all things. In our Western culture experiences, we don't fully appreciate the significance of certain scriptures nor fully understand or apply the truths to our lives. It's enriching to study, research, understand, and seek to know why people did what they did, and why Jesus said what He said, because it will help to uncover the truths that we can apply in our daily lives.

Matthew 18:1-6...Become As <u>This</u> Little Child

Jesus was speaking of being converted and coming as little children in order to enter into the Kingdom of Heaven. Matthew 18:4 declares, "Whosoever therefore shall humble himself <u>as this little child</u>, the same is greatest in the kingdom of heaven. And whoso shall receive one such little child in my name receiveth me."

To follow the entire context, we must look back to Matthew 18:1-2, which states, "At the same time came the disciples unto Jesus, saying, Who is the greatest in the kingdom of heaven? And Jesus called a little child unto him, and set him in the midst of them." Before Jesus answered the disciples' question, He called a little child to Himself. What was it about that particular child which is significant with regard to being the greatest in the Kingdom of Heaven? I believe the child took two significant actions which illustrate what Jesus desires in all of His children.

First, when Jesus called him, the child abandoned his position of security with his parents and friends and chose to go and be with Jesus. That is unusual for a little child, because they normally feel insecure and prefer to stay where they feel safe. The child had to leave his own place of security for the sake of identifying totally with Jesus. The child didn't know exactly where he was going or what he would be asked to do. He only knew that Jesus had called him, and he was going to Jesus!

Secondly, the child allowed Jesus to place him where He wanted him, and then he remained right there! Please note that according to verse 2, Jesus set the little child in the midst of them. After the child had responded to the call to come closer to Jesus, Jesus set him before the other people, and the child stayed where he was placed without feeling intimidated, fearful, embarrassed or self conscious. We must learn to patiently remain where Jesus places us until He gives us instruction to move on!

Matthew 21:6-7...We Must Deal with the Flesh

All three of the synoptic gospels record the account of Jesus' triumphal entry into Jerusalem several days prior to His crucifixion. Matthew 21:6-7 declares, "And the disciples went and did as Jesus commanded them, And brought the ass, and the colt, and put on them their clothes, and they set him thereon." I asked the Lord why the people put their garments on the animal before He sat upon him. The Lord quickened this thought to my spirit: *God will never, ever be glorified riding on flesh*. Our flesh must be dealt with if we are to glorify God in our lives!

Matthew 23:12...Humility

Jesus said, "And whosoever shall exalt himself shall be abased; and he that shall humble himself shall be exalted." It's clear in the study of the teaching of Jesus that no matter which direction we choose to go, we will end up humbled. We can either choose to humble ourselves or allow Him to do it! He was effectively saying, "I'll give you an opportunity to humble yourself, but if you ignore that opportunity, I'll take care of it for you!" This is a Kingdom principle.

An example of this principle in action occurred when Jesus and His apostles were in the upper room for the last supper. Peter was about to get a lesson in humility. Matthew 26:21:22 declares, "And as they did eat, he said, Verily I say unto you, that one of you shall betray me. And they were exceeding sorrowful, and began every one of them to say unto him, Lord, is it I?"

Please note that they all were sincere enough to realize they had the potential to betray Him even though they didn't have the desire to do so. We must be aware of that in our humanness. "Am I the one? Is it me? I don't desire to be the one, but is it me?" Peter was more vocal and less humble about it, and he effectively said, "Not me Lord! I will never ever deny you!" I wonder if he was thinking, "I'm not sure about these other guys, but I won't fail you. I've wondered about them from time to time, but I'm sure of myself." Of course, we know that Peter did indeed fail Jesus just a few hours after his outburst. Perhaps he should have taken the more humble, less vocal approach of his fellow apostles!

Matthew 25:1-13...Are You Sleeping?

One thing that has intrigued me about the parable of the wise and foolish virgins is that both the foolish and the wise virgins fell asleep. Matthew 25:5 states, "While the bridegroom tarried, they all slumbered and slept."

Even those that consider themselves sincerely committed to the Lord should take note that even the wise virgins were sleeping. Jesus was effectively saying that one sign of the end of the age is that even His church could be sleeping without even realizing that is the case.

I have observed three things that characterize sleep. First, we don't even know that we are asleep until we wake up. Secondly, we do some things in our dreams that we would never do if we were awake. Thirdly, we typically strongly dislike the sound of an alarm when we are asleep and we often reach for the snooze button. It behooves us to stay awake, responsive, alert, and sensitive to the direction and ministry of the Spirit of Lord in this day and hour.

Matthew 26:53...Twelve Legions of Angels

When the soldiers and officials came to arrest Jesus, Peter responded by pulling his sword and cutting off the servant's ear. Jesus restored the man's ear, but please hear the words of Jesus to Peter, who apparently had thought that his defense was in his own strength. Jesus' words are recorded in Matthew 26:53 which declares, "Thinkest thou that I cannot now pray to my Father, and he shall presently give me more than twelve legions of angels?"

A Roman legion was six thousand soldiers, so twelve legions of angels would be seventy-two thousand angels. In II Kings Chapter 19, Sennacherib's army came down to destroy Jerusalem at the time that Isaiah was prophet and Hezekiah was king. II Kings 19:35 declares, "And it came to pass that night, that the angel of the Lord went out, and smote in the camp of the Assyrians an hundred fourscore and five thousand Syrians."

If one angel can slay 185,000 people, basic mathematics tells us how many people twelve legions (72,000) angels can slay, and that number is a staggering 13,320,000,000! That's thirteen billion three hundred and twenty million, which is about double our world's population. Twelve legions of angels have the power to destroy every person on earth two times over. We serve a mighty God! Of course, we know that Jesus was not a helpless victim, but rather a victor, and He submitted Himself to crucifixion rather than call the angels at His disposal. Because He would not save Himself, you and I can be saved.

Matthew 26:74-75...A New Beginning

Jesus told Peter that he would deny Him three times before the cock crowed, and of course this came to pass as recorded in Matthew 26:74-75, "Then began he to curse and to swear, saying, I know not the man. And immediately the cock crew. And Peter remembered the word of Jesus, which said unto him, Before the cock crow, thou shalt deny me thrice. And he went out, and wept bitterly."

I asked the Lord why He used a cock, and not some other animal or method, as a signal and a sign to Peter. I believe that the Lord showed me it is because the cock was created to signal the dawn and thereby introduce a new day. When Peter was at his lowest point, God was effectively announcing, "It's not over Peter; it's simply the beginning of a new day, and dawn is coming." Of course at that time, Peter didn't know that in a few weeks he would preach his first sermon and three thousand people would be converted, but that sure sounds like dawn to me! Everything God does has meaning and purpose, and I believe that even the crowing of the cock has significance.

Matthew 28:19...Go Ye

Jesus was delivering what we call the Great Commission, and He said, "Go ye therefore, and teach all nations." That word "nations" is translated from the Greek word *ethnos* which means all ethnic groups, all ethnic peoples. Mark 16:15 relates the remainder of Jesus' commission, "And he said unto them, Go ye into all the world, and preach the gospel to every creature." Matthew's emphasis on this teaching is discipling all ethnic groups, and Mark's emphasis is preaching the gospel to every creature. The two fit like hand and glove.

One thing that impresses me in both of these expressions is the word <u>go</u> because in my experience in the church world, much of our appeal is in <u>coming</u> rather than going. I'm not in any way minimizing the importance of coming together and assembling as believers. Assembling is important in discipling, maturing, and growing strong and mighty in the Lord, but we must keep in mind that we are not to sit back passively, but instead aggressively reach out and touch others daily wherever God gives us opportunity. Remember that the commission is <u>go</u> ye. Go ye from where you are and from what you are doing. Go ye from the comfort of being at ease and saying "It's all up to God." God is surely involved, but as believers we have a "go ye" responsibility.

Matthew, Mark, Luke, and John...Different Perspectives

Please note all four of the gospel writer's descriptions of resurrection morning.

- Matthew declares in 28:1, "....as it began to dawn"

- Mark said in chapter 16 of his gospel, "....at the rising of the sun"
- Luke said in his gospel, chapter 24, "....very early in the morning"
- John wrote in chapter 20 of his gospel, "....when it was yet dark"

Bible skeptics focus on apparent contradictions like this and conclude that the Bible cannot be true because it contradicts itself. However, believers know that the Bible never contradicts itself. The perspective of Matthew, Mark, and Luke was that it was beginning to dawn, while John's perspective was that it was still dark. John was focusing on the dark, what was and still is. Matthew, Mark and Luke were focusing on the light, what was coming and shall be. They were looking at the same picture, the same event, but from a different perspective. It is important, I believe, at times like this to have the perspective, like the old proverb, of seeing the glass half full rather than half empty. Is it half empty or is it half full? It depends on whether you're thirsty or not!

Mark 4:35-41...Taking a Test

Mark Chapter 4 records the account of Jesus and the apostles in a boat on the Sea of Galilee. A storm arose, and Jesus was sleeping in the stern of the ship. Verse 35 records the beginning of this account, as it declares, "And the same day, when the even was come, he saith unto them, Let us pass over unto the other side." Please note Jesus' specific words to them.

He didn't say, "Let us go out in the water." He said, "Let us go to the other side."

Verse 36 states, "And when they had sent away the multitude, they took him even as he was in the ship, And there were also with him other little ships. And there arose a great storm of wind, and the waves beat into the ship, so that it was now full. And he was in the hinder part of the ship, asleep on a pillow; and they awake him, and say unto him, Master, carest thou not that we perish?"

Please note the apostles' sense of urgency and panic in this situation. They were hardy, seafaring men, and had likely tried every technique they knew of in order to deal with the storm, and yet they still feared for their lives. They finally got to the point at which they decided to cry out to Jesus and awaken Him. Please note that they called Him "Master" which means "teacher." They effectively said, "Teacher, don't you care that we are going to die? Teacher, say something, do something!" However, as we know, teachers never talk during a test, do they? That is because they want to see if their students learned the last lesson. Jesus had said, "We're going to the other side," so that was the last lesson the disciples had been taught, and now was the time for the test.

It is interesting that they called Him "Master" and not "Lord" here. They called Him "Teacher," but yet they hadn't learned the lesson. Have you ever been taking a test and you would like to have the teacher give you a little bit of help? If we apply that truth to our lives we'll find, on occasion, that the Word of the Lord comes to us and gives us instruction and direction. The opportunity comes to determine to what extent we heard, and acted upon, what He said. He is giving us a test!

Who is there among those in the ministry that hasn't endured some very tough days? I certainly have, and that is why I have compassion on pastors and teachers. Jesus never said it would be easy but He said it would be good, and there's a difference. We all have our tough Monday mornings, but each of those occasions is an opportunity to remember what Jesus said. He never fails. He cannot fail because He is God. Sometimes, we simply need to quiet ourselves and say, "Holy Spirit, remind us again of what You said. We want to be obedient because we know that the blessing of God comes when we're obedient." That is the highest way to declare His Lordship. We can sing or preach "He is Lord" until we have no more voice, but the ultimate proof of His Lordship in our lives is when we obey Him.

Mark 5:25-34...They Said, He Said

There are many truths in the story of the woman who had the issue of blood for twelve years, but let us look at a principle beyond her need for a physical change and a physical touch. The account begins in Mark 5:25, which declares, "And a certain woman, which had an issue of blood twelve years..."

The woman was obviously very sick and suffering a great deal. Leviticus 17:11 provides further insight which can be applied to this woman's situation when it states, "The life of the flesh is in the blood." Therefore, this woman wasn't just losing physical blood, she was losing life, and essentially losing her grip on life. We all walk through times, seasons, and situations that make it seem as if our grip on life is slipping away from us. When we find ourselves in such a circumstance, we can be encouraged that this woman's decision to pursue Jesus resulted in her being filled with His life, which had a healing and restoring power such that she was made whole.

Mark 5:26 declares, "And had suffered many things of many physicians, and had spent all that she had, and was nothing bettered, but rather grew worse." Please note that the fact that she pursued every means that she had available to help her did not disqualify her from the healing touch of Jesus. We must not condemn people that pursue other help until their healing manifests. There is a reason that the Holy Spirit puts everything in the Bible. That is neither unimportant nor insignificant. It's liberating to know that Jesus understands when we are dealing with our situations the best we can and seeking help and solutions. I see great mercy in our Lord.

As the account of this miracle healing comes to an end, verse Mark 5:33-35 states, "But the woman fearing and trembling, knowing what was done in her, came and fell down before him, and told him all the truth. And he said unto her, Daughter, thy faith hath made thee whole; go in peace, and be whole of thy plague. While he yet spake, there were some who came and said thy daughter is dead why troublest thou the Master any further?" Please note the phrase, "While he yet spake..." Let me interject that it's not a good idea to interrupt Jesus!

Please note that there are two voices here. Jesus is speaking faith, peace, and wholeness, but there is another voice speaking death and trouble. It is important for us to realize that when we are confronted with various situations in life, there are often multiple voices that we hear, and we must choose to whom we will listen. We must remember this: it's not what <u>they said</u> that's important; it's what <u>He said</u> that is important!

For example, Bartimaeus was sitting at the gate calling out for Jesus, and <u>they said</u> "Be quiet," but <u>He said</u> "Bring him to me." When Jesus arrived at the grave of Lazarus, <u>they said</u> "You're late, he's been dead for four days already," but <u>He said</u> "Roll thee away the stone." It's what He says that's important. It's what He says that matters. <u>They said</u>, "We caught her in the act of adultery." <u>He said</u>, "He that is without sin cast the first stone." <u>Phillip said</u>, "Two hundred penny worth is not enough" but <u>He said</u> "Make the people sit down."

Many times when we are in a difficult situation rather than running to the phone and finding out what "they said," we should run to the Word and find out what "He said!" If we ask twelve different people for advice, we could get twelve different answers. The more people we talk to, the more confused we may become. <u>They said</u> death and trouble, and <u>He said</u> peace and wholeness. We must focus on what He said!

Mark 8:22-25...Seeing Men as Trees

Jesus laid His hands on the eyes of a blind man and then asked the man, "What do you see?" The man replied, "I see men as trees walking." (Mark 8:24) Jesus then laid His hands on the man a second time, and this time his vision was totally healed. This is an interesting sequence of events, and the main question that arises in many of our minds is "Why wasn't the man completely healed the first time Jesus laid hands on him?"

I believe that this healing teaches us some valuable truths. For example, I believe that the first time when this man was touched by Jesus, he moved from darkness to light, which is consistent with God's work in our lives. When we are born again, we move from darkness to light, but we are often not ready to minister to people right away. We need more touches from Jesus before we can preach His word clearly, powerfully, and more compassionately.

The man saw "men as trees walking" after Jesus' first touch. However, after Jesus' second touch, the man no longer saw men as trees walking, but instead, he saw as Jesus saw. How might we interpret this idea of trees walking? First, let's consider the characteristics of trees. Trees are inanimate objects. They are things that we utilize to serve our needs. We build things from trees. We cut them down, saw them, plane them, carve them, and chisel them. However, people are not trees. In order to have the finished work of God in his life, this formerly blind man not only had to move from darkness to light (the first touch) but he also had to begin to see people like Jesus saw them (the second touch). He had to see people, not as inanimate objects, but rather as individuals that have hurts, pains, difficulties, and needs of all kinds, and who don't exist to serve our needs. We do not use people, we minister to people. They don't exist to serve us, but rather we exist to serve them. This man, after the second touch, saw like Jesus saw.

Jesus always saw with compassion and mercy. Whenever Jesus identified a problem, He healed it. When He identified demon powers, he broke the power of the demons. He didn't only expose issues, but He fixed them. Jesus had compassion because He saw like the Father saw. Whatever Jesus saw the Father do, He would do. When He looked at you and I at Calvary and He saw what we were and what we would become, He looked in love. He didn't look at us as something to be used. We are not inanimate objects. We are people that have life and have real needs.

It's the greatest miracle in all the world to lead somebody to Jesus, but that's not the end; it's just the beginning. I believe there is a process, a work, which God desires to do in our lives, and in the lives of everyone that He places in our care. The new birth is a wonderful beginning, and then it's our

Dr. Leonard Gardner

responsibility to make disciples of all men. Disciples means "disciplined ones," followers that would follow the way of the Lord and know the way of the Lord. The spirit of the world produces a "What can you do for me today?" mentality. It's a "gimme" consumer mentality in which "you exist to serve me and please me."

However, God's Spirit turns that mentality "right side up" and the Christian's motto becomes, "I exist to serve you, minister to you, and bless you." Jesus came to make all of us free and give us victory from being self-serving. This is a work that must transpire in all our lives as we go on with the Lord, but we can't begin that process until we have moved from darkness to light. The greatest miracle is being born again, but we need to allow the work of God in us to progress beyond being saved. We must not stop at the start!

Mark 15:22...The Place of a Skull

Mark 15:22 states, "And they bring him unto the place Golgotha, which is, being interpreted, The place of a skull."

In their gospels, both Matthew and John, describe the place of Jesus' crucifixion as Golgotha. The Book of Luke calls it Calvary, which is derived from the Latin as opposed to the Hebrew word. The names Golgotha and Calvary both mean "the place of a skull." It is true that the geography of the hill and the shaping of the rock resembles a skull, but I believe there is more meaning to "the place of a skull" than just geographical appearance. On the cross on that hill, called the place of a skull, Jesus fought the final battle and declared victory.

I believe that our biggest battle in our walk with the Lord is in our minds. The way we think, and the thoughts that we allow into our mind are crucial to our walk with God and our spiritual growth, maturity, and victory. Jesus cried out "It is finished!" at the place of a skull, announcing that He has given us victory in our thought lives and we can renew our minds in the Word of God. We can have victory in the place of our skull (our thought life)!

Luke 1:31...The Father Knew the Mission

The angel was delivering the word of the Lord to Mary and said, "And behold, thou shalt conceive in thy womb, and bring forth a son, and shalt call his name JESUS." In that day, the naming of children was very significant. Parents didn't simply choose a popular or nice-sounding name, but rather, they intended for the name to suggest something about the nature, character, or mission they foresaw for their child. I believe God the Father had to name Jesus because He is the only one that knew the mission. Mary didn't know the mission and neither did Joseph, her husband. God the Father knew the mission, so He effectively told Mary, "Not only will you conceive and bear a son, but you will call Him Jesus because He shall save His people from their sins." The Father named Jesus!

Luke 1:46...Rejoice in the Promise

"And Mary said, My soul doth magnify the Lord. And my spirit hath rejoiced in God my Savior." I think it is important and significant to all of us that she rejoiced in the <u>promise</u>, and she didn't wait until the <u>fulfillment</u> to rejoice. Let us rejoice in every promise of God, knowing that He is faithful. Don't wait for the fulfillment - rejoice now!

Luke 2:7...Laid in a Manger

Luke 2:7 states that Joseph and Mary laid the baby Jesus in a manger because there was no room for them in the Inn. I don't believe that Jesus being laid in a manger was an alternative, or God's "Plan B." I believe that Jesus being laid in a manger was every bit as much God's "Plan A" as Jesus being crucified on a cross. Jesus never is a victim. He was always the victor.

The Greek word translated "manger" is *phatne* and it refers to a trough where the choicest of foods and grains were given. The sheep spent much time in the pastures eating the grass of the fields, but every so often the shepherd would bring the sheep into the manger. When it was "manger time," it meant that the sheep were going to receive the very best quality food.

As recorded in John 6:31-41, Jesus said God had given the Hebrews manna in the wilderness, but He effectively said, "Now I am the bread of life, the bread from heaven." It is interesting to note that Jesus was born in Bethlehem of Judea, and the word Bethlehem" means "the house of bread." And, after His birth, they laid Him in the trough (the *phatne*), where the best food was provided to the sheep. Father sent Jesus, the choice Bread of Heaven, to the house of bread and placed Him in a quality trough. That sounds like Plan A to me!

If we don't realize this truth, we could otherwise assume that things somehow went wrong. Some may ask, "Who made the mistake that resulted in the need to lay Jesus in a manger...was it Joseph?" Joseph and Mary traveled for about eighteen days from Nazareth to Bethlehem to have the census taken. Didn't Joseph plan ahead and make lodging reservations? Or, some may wonder if perhaps the baby Jesus was born prematurely.

Of course, we know that Joseph did not make a mistake, nor was Jesus born prematurely. God's plan and timing are always perfect, and Jesus' birth occurred in the exact time and place according to God's perfect plan. Luke 2:6 declares, "...the days were accomplished that she should be delivered" and Galatians 4:4 states, "But when the fullness of the time was come, God sent forth his Son." The manger was not Plan B; it was Plan A. The Bread of Life came to the house of bread and was placed in the trough of the choicest bread. It was as if Father was saying to the world, "Here's the best that Heaven has to offer."

Dr. Leonard Gardner

The fact that there was no room for Him in the inn does not mean that God settled for second best. Father never makes a mistake. The timing and place of Jesus' birth was perfect. Jesus is not a victim. He is a victor!

Luke 6:6-11...Signs and Healings

During Jesus' earthly ministry, He healed hundreds, perhaps thousands, of people. On several occasions the phrase "...and He healed them all" is found in the Bible. However, the gospels only record about thirty of Jesus' healings. Why did the Lord select these particular healings to be recorded in His Word? I don't believe they are recorded to prove that Jesus is a healer. I believe He's a healer because He said He's a healer. His word is enough.

Why then did God select thirty healings to record in His Word? I believe that the answer is found in the Greek word *semeion* which is translated to the word "sign" in the New Testament. The thirty healings are signs that can point us to greater truths. Mark 16:17 declares, "These signs shall follow them that believe." The Greek word *semeion* refers to something which points to something greater than itself.

In studying the Word of God, we uncover truths and treasures which can be applied to practical areas of our lives, but which do not in any way diminish the importance of the literal interpretation of scripture. I want to emphasize that I believe that every miracle happened exactly the way the Bible says it did. However, God selected the thirty specific miracles that He wanted to record because they are *semeions*, signs which point to deeper truths. When we study the Bible, we should ask the Holy Spirit to reveal to us the deeper truths and principles. Proverbs 25:2 states, "It is the glory of God to conceal a thing; but the honour of kings to search out a matter."

For example, when we search out the deeper truths and principles in Jesus' healing of the man with the withered hand (Luke 6:6-11), we can observe four things of note which we can apply in our lives.

The first thing of note is the word <u>withered</u> itself, because "withered" means "to lose vitality, power, shape, function, or freshness." Something that is withered is not what it used to be and/or it is less than it should be. This is not limited to a part of our physical bodies. It can be anything that is prone to wither or wane, such as our prayer life, our love for the Lord, or our compassion for others. *We can have withered parts of our physical or spiritual lives that are simply not what they used to be or should now be.* The second thing of note is that it was the man's <u>right hand,</u> which in scripture signifies authority. *When Jesus called this man, he submitted immediately to the authority of Jesus.*

The third and fourth things of note are two statements that Jesus made to the man which are significant. He said, "Stand forth" and "Stretch forth." When Jesus instructed the man to "Stand forth," He was effectively telling him to go up in front of all the other guests. When He said "Stretch forth," the man had to extend the withered area of his life for all to see. If a person has one hand that is withered and one that is not, he would much rather stretch out the good one. Jesus asked him to reveal, unveil, and acknowledge that area that is less than it used to be and not what it should be. *In order for Jesus to heal our withered areas, we must be humble and bold enough to stand forth and stretch forth our withered areas so that He can heal it!*

Luke 6:36-38...The Law of Reciprocity

"Be ye therefore merciful, as your Father also is merciful; Judge not, as ye shall not be judged; condemn not, and ye shall not be condemned; forgive, and ye shall be forgiven; Give, and it shall be given unto you; good measure, pressed down, and shaken together."

One important principle in the Kingdom of God is called the law of reciprocity. In short, it means that we receive back in the same measure and kind that we give. So in effect, we prophecy our own future by our actions. For example, if we don't forgive, we are therefore prophesying that we won't be forgiven. If we don't honor, we are prophesying we won't be honored. Not only is the law of reciprocity prophetic, but it is also just as real as the law of gravity in the natural world. What we do is not trivial or unimportant; it all will affect us in some way, shape, or form. We may think our actions only affect others, but they also affect ourselves. When we realize that what we do will come back around, and that we are essentially prophesying our own future by our actions, we will likely be much more careful about the decisions we make and the actions we take!

Luke 9:51-56...Don't Proof-Text!

"And it came to pass, when the time was come that he should be received up, he steadfastly set his face to go to Jerusalem, And sent messengers before his face; and they went, and entered into a village of the Samaritans, to make ready for him. And they did not receive him, because his face was as though he would go to Jerusalem. And when his disciples, James and John saw this, they said, Lord, wilt thou that we command fire to come down from heaven, and consume them even as Elias <Elijah> did?"

The phrase that caught my attention is "even as Elijah did." (Luke 9:54) It is true that Elijah did indeed call fire down from heaven to consume sinners (II Kings 1:10-14). However, simply because Elijah did it didn't mean that the Lord wanted James and John to do it in their specific situation! James and John were effectively saying, "We want to destroy these people and we have scripture to support our position. We have a precedent which we can cite. Elijah called down fire, so we should be

Dr. Leonard Gardner

able to do it as well." We call this "proof-texting" in the ministry world. It's human nature to think along these lines, but we must beware of the mentality that says, "We already know what we believe (or want to believe) and we're going to find scripture to support our view!" We must be careful not to proof-text in our lives and in our ministries!

Luke 10:17-19...Serpents and Scorpions

When the seventy returned from the ministry trip on which Jesus had sent them He said to them, "Behold, I give unto you power to tread on serpents and scorpions, and over all the power of the enemy; and nothing shall by any means hurt you." (Luke 10:19)

Every word that Jesus spoke is important, and because He specifically mentioned serpents and scorpions, we should endeavor to understand more about these creatures. Jesus said that He would give us power over both serpents and scorpions, so let's examine the characteristics of both. Most of us are somewhat familiar with serpents, particularly the fact that many of them are venomous and, if given the opportunity, they will inject their venom (poison) into their victims. They will "put something into" their victims that can destroy the person unless an antidote is administered.

Many of us aren't as familiar with the characteristics of scorpions, but it is interesting to note that the way that scorpions kill is somewhat the opposite of the way serpents kill. Scorpions first inject their target with a numbing fluid which causes the tissue to die, and they then literally suck the tissue from the helpless victim.

Please note this contrast - while serpents <u>put something in you</u> that will destroy you, scorpions <u>take something out of you</u> that you need. Scorpions remove once healthy and living tissue from their victims. Serpents "inject death" and scorpions "extract life." Jesus gave the seventy, and us as well, power over both of these "attack strategies" of the devil. Jesus effectively said, "I give you power to prevent the enemy from injecting death into you, and I also give you power to prevent the enemy from extracting life, such as love, joy, and peace, from you." In Christ, we can handle anything we face. We have power regardless of how the devil chooses to attack. We have power over both serpents and scorpions!

Luke 15:11-32...The Father's Love

The prodigal son "came to himself" (we might say that he came to his senses), and began to rehearse the speech he was going to give to his father when he arrived at his father's house. Luke 15:18 states, "I will arise and go to my father, and will say unto him, Father, I have sinned against heaven, and before thee. And am no more worthy to be called thy son; make me as one of thy hired servants."

When the son eventually arrived at his father's house, he began his rehearsed speech. Luke 15:21 declares, "And the son said unto him, Father, I have sinned against heaven, and in thy sight, and am no more worthy to be called thy son. But the father said..." Note that the father interrupted the son, who didn't have the opportunity to finish his speech, specifically the part which said, "....make me as one of thy hired servants."

The father wouldn't let him speak that way. He effectively said, "You are not going to be a hired servant; you are still my son." Aren't you glad that God the Father doesn't let us "finish our speech?" Aren't you glad there are some prayers He doesn't answer? The prodigal son felt badly for his sins. He simply wanted to do what he felt was right to make up for his sins, but he didn't understand the love and forgiveness of the father. He didn't understand that the father loved him even before he left, and forgave him even before he left. The son was coming back into open, welcoming arms. I can just imagine this father getting up every morning, peering out over the hillside and thinking, "Perhaps today is the day my son comes back to me." That's the only way I can explain how the father saw the son while he was far off. The son didn't get the opportunity to say, "Dad, I just want to be a hired hand." Father was waiting for him and had better things in mind for his wayward son!

Luke 15:11-32...In the Family but Not in the House

The elder son had issues of his own. Luke 15:28 states, "And he was angry, and would not go in; therefore came his father out, and entreated him."

His dad literally begged him to come into the house. What was in the house that his father wanted him to have? First, there was joy, because there was singing and dancing in the house. Secondly, there was food (provision) in the house because they had killed the fatted calf. Incidentally, I believe that one reason the elder son was angry was because they were eating the calf he had fatted (fed). Thirdly, the presence of the father was in the house. I believe there is a cry from the heart of our Father to people that are in the family but aren't in the house. We have all been given the invitation, and our Father says "Come on into the house where you will find joy, provision, and My presence." God wants us, not only in the family, but also in the house!

Luke 15:11-32...Six Signs of Unforgiveness

In the parable of the prodigal son, we often focus on the younger son or the father, but there are also important truths and principles to be learned from observing the actions and words of the elder son. Perhaps the elder son ended up in a worse condition than the younger because he was dealing with the matter of unforgiveness. We all understand the importance of forgiveness. In His teachings, Jesus said that there are two conditions which must be satisfied when we come to Him in prayer. One is that we believe (James 1:16) and the other is that we forgive (Matthew 18:35). Forgiveness is vitally important.

I believe that the elder son held unforgiveness toward his brother for what he felt his brother had done, and also toward his father because his father forgave his brother.

Nonetheless, the father went out of the house and implored his elder son to come into the house. The elder son made six statements in his response to the father that indicates he had not forgiven his brother nor his father. We know that the Lord places importance on forgiveness, and I believe that we all want to walk in forgiveness and experience it in our lives. We want to be faithful to forgive, but we also know that Jeremiah 17:9 states that man's heart "is deceitful above all things and desperately wicked; who can know it?" We should not only be interested in saying "I forgive" in our heads, but we should also want to know in our hearts that we have forgiven.

I believe there are six things in the elder son's statements which we can use to evaluate ourselves to determine if we are walking in unforgiveness. The first three are found in Luke 15:29 and the second three are found in Luke 15:30.

Principle #1: Unforgiveness keeps score. Verse 29 states, "And he answering said to his father, Lo, these many years do I serve thee." Peter asked Jesus how many times we should forgive someone who wrongs us. Jesus answered, "Seventy times seven," but He was effectively saying that there is no limit...we must never keep score.

Principle #2: Unforgiveness boasts of its own record. The elder son said, "...neither transgressed I at any time thy commandment." When we boast of our own record rather than being humble, we are walking in unforgiveness.

Principle #3: Unforgiveness complains that it's not fair. The elder son said, as recorded in verse 29, "...and yet thou never gavest me a kid." By all human standards, it may indeed seem unfair that the elder son never got an animal to roast for a feast with his friends. However, it may be that this statement reveals that he was so focused on blessings from the father that he wasn't putting proper emphasis on the blessing of the father, that is, being in the presence of the father. Our Lord not only blesses us, but He Himself is the highest blessing we could ever receive.

Principle #4: Unforgiveness alienates. The elder son said, "But as soon as this thy son was come..." The elder son referred to his brother as "thy son" rather than "my brother." When we are harboring unforgiveness, we alienate ourselves from others and distance ourselves from relationships.

Principle #5: Unforgiveness always thinks of a person as they were, not as they are. The elder son said of his brother, "....which hath devoured thy living with harlots." In this exchange, the elder son was the only one that said anything about harlots.

The father didn't bring up the harlots and neither did the younger son. The elder son made it a point to bring up the past sins of his brother to the father.

<u>Principle #6: Unforgiveness becomes angry when others are blessed</u>. The elder son said, "....thou hast killed for him the fatted calf." He was effectively saying, "You killed for him the calf I fed. I've been here taking care of that calf all along. I'm the one that fattened the calf and my brother's enjoying it." Our Father sends rain on the just and the unjust (Matthew 5:45), and we must accept that truth. Romans 2:4 states that it is the goodness of God that leads to repentance.

Luke 17:11-19...Jesus Wants Us To Be Whole!

The account of the healing of the ten lepers is recorded in Luke 17:11-19. Verses 11-14 declare, "And it came to pass, as he went to Jerusalem that he passed through the midst of Samaria and Galilee. And as he entered into a certain village, there met him ten men that were lepers, which stood afar off; And they lifted up their voices, and said, Jesus, Master, have mercy on us. And when he saw them, he said unto them, Go shew yourselves unto the priests, And it came to pass, that, as they went, they were cleansed."

The Greek word translated "cleansed" is *katharizo* and it means "purged or purified." Under the law, lepers they had to be declared clean in order to go back into society so Jesus was submitting to the law of that day. Lepers would show themselves to the priest so that he could verify their healing, and he then would ceremonially cleanse them by applying the blood on their right earlobe, right thumb, and right toe. Then he applied the oil (a type of the Holy Spirit).

After their cleansing, Luke 17:15-18 states, "And one of them, when he saw that he was healed, turned back, and with a loud voice glorified God. And fell down on his face at his feet, giving him thanks; and he was a Samaritan. And Jesus answering said, Were there not ten cleansed? But where are the nine? There are not found that returned to give glory to God, save this stranger."

The ten lepers were healed (the Greek word *iaomai* means "cured"), but only one returned to Jesus to thank Him, and that one was not only healed, purified, and purged, but he was about to receive even more.

This passage is often preached with a focus placed on the importance of giving thanks for what God does. I certainly believe that we need to be not only givers of thanks, but also thankful. We give thanks as an action, but thankfulness is a condition - it means that we are full of thanks! Scripture consistently teaches that we ought to be thankful, but I believe there is another truth in this account of the lepers which we can learn and apply to our lives.

Dr. Leonard Gardner

I believe that the heart of Jesus was not so much to scold the nine for not coming back and expressing their thanks as it was a cry of compassion, in which He was effectively saying, "There are nine men walking around out there that have had the blood applied but who are not whole." Only one leper came back and fell before Jesus to express his gratitude. Luke 17:19 declares, "And Jesus answering said, Were there not ten cleansed? But where are the nine? And he said unto him, Arise, go thy way; thy faith hath made thee whole."

Please note that this one leper had not only been healed, but also made whole! The Greek word *sozo* that is translated "whole" refers to the provision of God for the whole man, spirit, soul and body. The cry of the heart of Jesus was not only for the one that was made whole, but for the nine that didn't receive everything from Him that he wanted them to have. There were nine men walking around out there with less than they needed. Yes, they had been granted permission to return to society, and they had the blood applied, and those things are extremely important. However, God's desire is that we not only have the blood applied (be saved), but also that we go beyond that and we become whole in spirit, soul and body (become whole and complete in Him).

Therefore, I see the question, "Where are the nine?" as not so much a question of rebuke as a question of compassion. Somewhere out there were nine men that had the blood and oil applied, but after receiving all of that by grace, the men didn't lay their lives at the feet of Jesus and become truly whole.

Luke 19:1-10...Who is the Greater Sinner?

I write about the account of Zacchaeus, which is recorded in Luke 19:1-10, in my book entitled "The Unfeigned Love of God." When the people standing there saw Zacchaeus, the stored-up anger they had inside of them for this hated tax collector likely began to boil over. They were likely surprised that Jesus had called this wretched man, and even more surprised that Zacchaeus had responded to Jesus' invitation and that Jesus would go to the house of such a sinful man! "What? Jesus is going to Zacchaeus' house?" While Jesus and Zacchaeus were going to the house, Luke 19:7 states, "And when they saw it, they all murmured, saying, That he was gone to be guest with a man that is a sinner."

When I was meditating on this scripture, I felt the Holy Spirit say to me, "That's interesting, they must have thought their murmuring was not a sin." They were judging, condemning and murmuring because of Zaccheus' past sins, but they could not see that what they were doing themselves was also sin! They were in effect saying, "Your sin is bad and my sin is not so bad." Who then was the greater sinner? We must be very careful in judging others!

John 1:1-5...Darkness and Light

Between the Old and New Testaments, there were four hundred years of silence, of "total darkness." During this dark and silent period of history, God didn't speak and no one heard the Word. For *four hundred years* there had been spiritual darkness and then the light of Jesus came and dispelled the darkness.

John writes in John 1:1-5, "In the beginning was the Word, and the Word was with God, and the Word was God. The same was in the beginning with God. All things were made by him; and without him was not any thing made that was made. In him was life; and the life was the light of men. And the light shineth in darkness; and the darkness comprehended it not."

John 1:5 is sometimes not clearly understood because of the word which is translated as "comprehended." However, this is a very powerful verse when the Greek verb tenses are taken into account and the word is more accurately translated as "overcome." John 1:5 can be accurately translated, "And the light shines and keeps on shining in the darkness, and the darkness has not, cannot, and will never overcome the light." Jesus came, and His light will forever overcome and dispel the darkness!

John 1:23...A Voice, Not an Echo

John the Baptist identified himself by saying, "I am the voice of one crying in the wilderness, Make straight the way of the Lord, as said the prophet Esaias (Isaiah)."

Did you ever hear yourself praying and you heard something that didn't go through your conscious mind? The Apostle Paul wrote that sometimes we pray with the understanding and sometimes we pray with the spirit. One day, a number of years ago, I heard myself praying "Lord, make me a voice and not an echo" and I thought to myself, "That is interesting. What did I mean by that?"

I began to study the differences between a voice and an echo. An echo sounds very much like the voice. It has the same pronunciation, diction, and accent. However, the Lord said to me, "An echo doesn't have the breath in it." We can say the right thing at the right time in the right way, but if there is no breath in it (the Holy Spirit), then there is no power in what we say, and it is just an empty echo which lacks effectiveness. The importance is not only in the preparation of the word we preach but more so in the preparation of the preacher that preaches it. We can say all the right things and say them exactly as someone else said them, but it doesn't have the same impact because it doesn't have the breath in it. It's the breath, the anointing of the Holy Spirit, that makes it effective.

John the Baptist was sent to be a voice, not an echo. He

Dr. Leonard Gardner

spoke the truth of the Holy Spirit, and his message was tremendously effective in changing lives.

John 1:37-42...A Stone and the Rock

My book entitled "Chosen to Follow Jesus" examines each of the twelve disciples and the recorded accounts in the Bible of their interactions with Jesus. It follows their lives all the way to their deaths as they were recorded in written tradition. Jesus prayed to the Father and specifically chose each of His apostles...they were indeed chosen to follow Jesus. Likewise, He also says to us, "You have not chosen me but I have chosen you." He has chosen every one of us out of the world, just as He chose His apostles, and therefore we can learn much that will help us in our walk with God by studying the lives of the apostles.

John 1:37-42 records the account of Andrew coming to Jesus. At that time, Andrew had known Jesus for about a year because Andrew had been a disciple of John the Baptist. When Andrew came to Jesus, he immediately went to his brother Simon (Peter) and brought him to Jesus. As a side note, that's a great principle for us to apply to our lives - we must realize that our ministry starts with our own family. We might think that family and close friends are the toughest to evangelize because they know all of our faults, but I think we can safely say that Simon Peter knew all about Andrew but he still came to Jesus.

Andrew brought him to Jesus and, John 1:42 states, "And when Jesus beheld him, he said, Thou art Simon, the son of Jona; thou shalt be called Cephas, which is by interpretation, A stone."

Please note that Jesus didn't say "the stone," "the rock," or "a rock." He said, "a stone." I learned from a geologist that there is a distinct difference between a stone and a rock. A stone generally only has one mineral but a rock has more than one mineral. Therefore, a stone isn't necessarily a piece of the rock, it's distinct. It has many of the same characteristics but there is a difference. And, of course, there is a very big difference between Peter and Jesus. Peter was a stone, but Jesus is the rock! You can't build upon a stone, but you can build upon the rock! Jesus said, "....upon this rock will I build my church; and the gates of hell shall not prevail against it."

John 1:51...Verily, Verily

In this verse, as well as several other places in his gospel, John records that Jesus began speaking by using the introductory phrase, "Verily, verily." The synoptic gospel writers use the single word "verily" but that word is actually a transliteration of the Hebrew meaning "truth" or "of a truth." The transliteration of the Greek word into English is "amen." Jesus was the only one that could say amen before He said what He was going to say because He never said anything that wasn't true. Sometimes as preachers, we have to "amen" ourselves due to the absence of "amens" from others! So it is with Jesus - He would say effectively "Amen, amen," and then He would say what He was going to say.

Early in Jesus' earthly ministry, at the Mount of Transfiguration (Matthew 17), Father looked down upon Him and said "This is my beloved Son, in whom I am well pleased; hear ye him." The Father was confident in telling us to listen to Jesus before He said anything, because Jesus never said anything that He didn't hear the Father say. Jesus always speaks 100% truth and we can trust Him and we can say in our heart "Amen, amen" every time we are about to receive His Word through Bible study, prayer, or a preached message. We must make up our mind to agree with every word that proceeds from the mouth of God. Amen, amen!

John 2:1-11...Following Mary's Example

John 2:1-11 records the account of a wedding celebration in Cana which Jesus and Mary both attended. The hosts had run out of wine, so they went to Mary to ask her what they should do about their problem. Mary said these words as recorded in John 2:5, "Whatsoever he saith unto you do it." It is interesting that these are the last recorded words in the Bible that Mary spoke. One of the privileges I had as the pastor of a church was that God sent many people to us that, through their personal experience, had been taught to honor Mary and pray to her. I certainly believe we should honor Mary as a wonderful

Treasures in the Word Volume 1

woman and servant of God, but some of the people in my congregation were having a great deal of difficulty not praying to Mary. The Lord showed me what I was to say to these precious people. He told me that the greatest way to honor Mary is do what she told us to do. She told the people at Cana to talk to Jesus! She directed them to speak to the One who knows all things and can do all things. The last thing recorded in the Bible that Mary effectively said was, "Talk to Him. He can do anything. He cares about your situation. He has everything under control and can solve any problem. Talk to Jesus!"

John 4:1-42...Jacob's Well

John 4:1-42 records the account of Jesus encountering a woman at a well in Samaria. John 4:6 states, "Now Jacob's well was there, Jesus therefore, being wearied with his journey, sat thus on the well; and it was about the sixth hour." Please note that this encounter took place at "Jacob's well." Jacob can best be described as a "rascal" and Jacob's well is therefore a type of the old nature (the sinful nature of man). We all struggle from time to time with our old nature, and if the truth be told, there's a little bit of rascal in every one of us.

A big part of this woman's problem was that she was living out of Jacob's well, which, spiritually speaking, refers to living out of the old nature. She returned repeatedly to Jacob's well to draw out of the old nature. Even as believers who have been given a new nature by God, we sometimes find ourselves in situations where we return to living out of our old nature. When we make that mistake, Jesus, by His grace, will "sit on our well" and hinder us from going back to the old nature, for our own good. Instead of trying to circumvent Jesus to get to Jacob's well, we must allow Him to change our nature by receiving the living water that He desires to give us so that we live out of the new nature and not out of the old nature!

John 5:1-16...Lacking Power

The lame man at the pool of Bethesda had been there for thirty-eight years. The Bible uses the word "impotent" (which means "lacking power") to describe the man. One day, the <u>omnipotent</u> came face to face with the <u>impotent</u>, and the <u>all powerful</u> one met the one <u>lacking power</u>.

Jesus asked the lame man, "Wilt thou be made whole?" We know that Jesus is perfect and does everything with purpose. Why then did He ask a man that had been lame for thirty-eight years if he wanted to be whole? That may seem like an obvious question, but we know that whenever God asks a question it's never because He needs more information. One of God's attributes is omniscience, which means that He knows everything about everything. He doesn't lack knowledge. When He asks a question it is so that we can hear what is in our own hearts by the content of our answer. Our answer will reveal to us what's in our own heart. It's as if He is placing a mirror in front of us in the form of a question.

What was the lame man's answer to Jesus' question? He effectively said, "I have two problems. First, when the water is troubled, I have no one to put me into the pool. It's their fault, not mine! Secondly, someone always beats me to it and therefore he gets healed and I don't."

If having no helper was really the man's issue, perhaps Jesus would have asked one of His disciples to stay with the man and help him into the pool the next time the water was stirred. However, Jesus didn't even address this because that wasn't the issue. Jesus was trying to allow the man to hear his own heart. The man's answer revealed that he had been lying there all the time thinking, "Nobody cares about me."

The second thing the man effectively said was, "When the water is troubled somebody always gets there before me." In other words, "It's not fair. Life's not fair!" We must learn that although things don't seem fair to us, we must not use that as an excuse for the "impotence" (the lack of power) in our lives.

The man was lame (impotent) for thirty-eight years. I believe that every time the name of a person, the name of a place, or a number is recorded in the Bible, it has significance. Therefore, I sought the Lord regarding the significance of the thirty-eight years. A long period of time passed before I received the answer to my question. Then, one day I saw in Deuteronomy

Dr. Leonard Gardner

2:14 that the children of Israel who listened to the ten spies' negative report at Kadesh-Barnea wandered for thirty-eight years until they all died. I concluded that because the children of Israel had an attitude of doubt and refused to believe God's promise, they wandered in the wilderness for thirty-eight years. They wandered with a lack of power in their lives for thirty-eight years! Likewise, the man at the pool of Bethesda spent thirty-eight years living below the level God wanted him to live, lacking power in his life, because of his attitude.

John 8:2-11...Case Closed!

This is the account of the woman taken in adultery. When Jesus said, "He that is without sin among you, let him first cast a stone at her" (John 8:7), He was clearly the only one in the entire crowd qualified to throw a stone, yet He wouldn't do so, and His words caused her accusers to drop their stones and leave the area.

Verses 10-11 record the interaction between Jesus and the woman after the others had left. Jesus said, "....where are those thine accusers? Hath no man condemned thee?" She said No man, Lord." Please note that she called him "Lord." It is always significant to note when He is referred to as "Jesus" or "Master" or "Lord" because it provides a glimpse into how the person views Jesus. Jesus went on to say to the woman, "....Neither do I condemn thee; go, and sin no more."

Jesus could have said, "Neither do I condemn thee, sin no more" but he included the word "go" in His instruction to her. I began to research the word "go" and I discovered that there are approximately thirty different Greek words that are translated into the English word "go" in the New Testament. In John 8:11, the Greek word *poreuomai* is used, and the original oriental usage of this word indicates "the close of a case in court, the formal end of a debate." In colloquial language, we might say, "This is over. This case is closed. It is time to move on. Don't park here."

Deuteronomy 2:3 declares that God said to the children of Israel, "Ye have compassed this mountain long enough; turn you northward." The mountain referred to in this verse is Mount Seir which means "rough." God was effectively saying, "You've circled this rough place long enough. Now move on and go to where you are going." The enemy will try to keep us going in circles around the rough places we encounter in life, but we must learn to say, "I am not staying here. I am moving on. This case is closed!" The original usage of the Greek word *poreuomai* implies that the judge won't even entertain the thought of the case being brought up in the court again. It is effectively erased off the books, as if it never happened. That's the deeper meaning of the word "go" that Jesus spoke to the woman caught in adultery. He was setting her free from the rough place, and we must allow Him to do the same for us!

Dr. Leonard Gardner

John 11:44...God Allows Us to Participate in His Miracles

When Jesus dispatched His disciples to fetch the little colt on which He would make His triumphal entry into Jerusalem, He effectively said, "If you are encountered by someone asking what are you doing loosing the colt, tell him the master hath need of him." (Matthew 21:3) He was essentially saying that the creator of all things needed this colt.

We know that Jesus didn't need this particular colt simply because He didn't have any others from which to choose. God could have created another colt on the spot. The Spirit could have transported Jesus into Jerusalem without the need for any earthly mode of transportation at all. Jesus didn't need the colt out of His lack; He needed him out of His love. He was saying in effect, "I am going to include that little colt in the glory, the miracle, that's going to be manifest today. I choose to need him. I love him so much that I choose to need him."

John Chapter 11 contains the account of the raising of Lazarus. Why did Jesus, who was all powerful and who had just raised Lazarus from the grave, ask the disciples to unwrap Lazarus from his grave clothes? (John 11:44) If Jesus had enough power to raise him from the dead, He of course had enough power to bring him out unwrapped! Jesus can do anything, but once again, He involved the disciples in the miracle and allowed them to participate. I sometimes feel like the disciples at Lazarus' grave may have felt when I preach and people come to

Jesus. I realize that He is performing the greatest miracle of all - saving souls - and he graciously allows me the privilege of participating in the miracle.

When we begin to realize how the Lord allows us to be a part of His plan and purpose on the earth, serving Him will never again seem like a burden, problem or weight, but rather a joy and a privilege! He loves us so much that He lets us in on His miracles!

John 21:1-19 records the account of when the fishermen fished all night and caught nothing. Jesus stood on the shore the next morning and said "How many fish have you caught out there without Me?" To fishermen, the only thing worse than not catching fish is admitting it, but they answered, "Well, we have fished all night and we have caught nothing." Jesus said, "Cast the nets on the right side." He didn't say "the other side," He said "the right side." (Is that right as opposed to left or right as opposed to wrong? Something to ponder!)

When they cast the nets on the right side of the boat, they brought in a tremendous catch of fish. Then, when they finally got that haul into shore they saw Jesus already had fish which He was cooking over a fire! He let them in on the miracle because there is nothing more thrilling to a fisherman than seeing his nets teeming with fish.

If it was only a matter of catching fish, Jesus could have simply commanded the fish to jump directly into the boat because there is nothing impossible with Jesus. He can do all things, but He loves us so much that He "chooses to need us." The King of the Universe, the Lord of Glory, the Creator of all Things, says that we have been chosen to be involved in the manifestation of His purposes. It's absolutely amazing! If we embrace that truth in our hearts, we will never grapple about being involved in the Lord's work. It is truly a privilege.

John 12:1-11...Don't Let the Thief Take Your Gift

Mary anointed the feet of Jesus with a very expensive ointment called spikenard. There were those present that night in Bethany who became very upset with her actions, one of which was Judas Iscariot. John 12:5 states that Judas asked, "Why was not this ointment sold for three hundred pence, and given to the poor?" The next verse states, "This he said, not that he cared for the poor; but because he was a thief, and had the bag, and bare what was put therein." Judas was a thief, and that's why he complained about what Mary did with the ointment.

Mary walked into the room bearing a gift that night and walked right by Judas. She refused to give her gift to the thief but instead desired to give her gift to Jesus. We all have gifts, abilities, talents, and anointings, and we have a choice to whom we will give them. Will we pour our gifts out on Jesus or let the thief take them from us? We must not let the thief take that which belongs to Jesus!

John 20:1-10...The Lesson of the Folded Napkin

In his gospel, John recorded something that none of the other gospel writers recorded with respect to the events that happened the morning of Jesus' resurrection. John recorded that when Peter went into the empty tomb, he saw something that the others didn't see - the folded napkin. (John 20:6-7) The closer we get to Jesus the more we will see! The napkin was the cloth that had been wrapped around the head of Jesus after His death.

The folded napkin relates two significant truths. The first and perhaps the most obvious truth it illustrates is that the work of the Head is finished. Jesus is the Head of the church, His spiritual body, and His work is done. He proclaimed from the cross "It is finished!"

To appreciate the second truth of the folded napkin, we must understand a Jewish tradition in which, particularly in a wealthy household, the master of the house would communicate to his servant by way of the napkin on the table. As the servant prepared the master's meal, the master was not present in the room. When the meal was finally all prepared, the servant would notify the master that his meal was ready. The servant would leave the room and the master would enter, sit down, and begin to eat.

One of two things could then occur: either the master would finish the meal and depart, or he would leave the room temporarily with the intention of returning to finish his meal. The master would communicate his intention by way of the napkin. If the master had finished eating, he would simply take the napkin and throw it on the table unfolded and in a haphazard fashion. However, if he was not finished and was coming back, he would neatly fold the napkin and leave it lying on the table. After the master left, the servant would then enter and look at the napkin. When the servant saw a folded napkin, he knew the master was effectively saying, "I'm coming back."

Peter went into the empty tomb and saw the folded napkin, and he preached passionately after Jesus' ascension, effectively saying, "This same Jesus whom ye crucified, is coming back. Don't let anybody tell you otherwise. The napkin's folded, He's coming back!"

John 21:15-17...Love and Relationship

My book entitled "Eight Principles of Abundant Living" examines the eight miracles recorded in the Gospel of John, seven of which occurred before the crucifixion and one of which occurred after the resurrection. The book brings to light important principles that each of those eight miracles teach us. John 21:15-17 records the account of the restoration and recommissioning of Peter by Jesus. The Lord asked Peter three times if he loved Him. In His first two questions to Peter, the word "love" is translated from the Greek word *agape*, which means "the act of love" and is sometimes described as "deep, unconditional love; the God kind of love." Peter answered Jesus on both occasions using a different word for "love", specifically the word *phileo*, which means "friendly, human, affectionate brotherly love." Jesus had asked Peter twice if he "*agape'd*" Jesus, and Peter answered both times that he "*phileo'd*" Jesus!

Jesus, ever understanding, kind, and patient, met Peter where he was after Peter's second *phileo* response and with His third question, Jesus effectively said, "Peter, do you *phileo* me?" Peter effectively responded, "Lord, you know that I *phileo* you." God desires that we love Him deeply with *agape* love, but sometimes He will ask us questions or place us in situations which help us to honestly and clearly see the level of love we have for Him in our hearts. Do we *phileo* Him or truly *agape* Him?

John 21:15-17...Feeding and Nurturing the Lambs

Jesus' instructions to Peter's three responses were as follows: first, "Feed My lambs," secondly, "Feed My sheep," and thirdly, "Feed My sheep." Please note that Jesus used the word "lambs" in His first response and the word "sheep" in His last two responses.

In Jesus' first response, the word translated "feed" is the Greek word *bosko,* which means "to provide food and nourishment." Jesus was effectively saying, "Will you feed My little lambs?"

In Jesus' second response, the word translated "feed" is the Greek word *poimaino,* which means "to nurture, to train, to bring to maturity." Lambs in particular need nurturing to grow into mature sheep to be able to function in adult lives as adult sheep. Therefore, Jesus was effectively saying, "Nurture my sheep."

In His third response, Jesus again used the word *bosko* meaning, "I want you to provide my sheep with food and nourishment."

Therefore, sheep need both food and nurturing, and our calling as pastors and leaders is twofold: to <u>feed</u> and <u>nurture</u> the sheep which God has entrusted to us. We provide them with food and nourishment through preaching and teaching the Word of God. We nurture them through care, compassion, and counsel.

Acts 3:1-11…The Importance of Discipleship

Many times when we preach the account of the healing of the lame man at the Gate Beautiful, we end our teaching with Acts 3:6, which states, "Such as I have give I thee; In the name of Jesus Christ of Nazareth rise up and walk." However, the writer of the Book of Acts, Luke, didn't finish the story there! Acts 3:7 declares, "And he took him by the right hand, and lifted him up; and immediately his feet and ankle bones received strength."

For a number of seconds or perhaps minutes, this man who had been touched by God's grace was living off of the strength of someone (Peter) who had ministered to him. Peter took the man by the hand and lifted him up, and immediately <u>after</u> he lifted him up, the strength came into his ankle bones and he began to walk. The strength didn't come until <u>after</u> Peter lifted him up, <u>not before</u>. I believe this speaks about the importance of not only ministering to people in miracle power but also discipling people. Unless we commit our time and energy to stay right there with believers that are young in the faith, we haven't fulfilled the commission of Jesus when He effectively said, "Go into all the world and make disciples of all men." (Matthew 28:19) Like Peter, we must lift them up and hold them until they can walk, run, jump, and shout on their own.

Sometimes it is difficult to get people committed to discipleship because it's not glamorous. Discipling people can require a significant commitment of strength, energy, patience, and time. It requires us to give of ourselves to help another get on his or her feet, and then the Holy Spirit immediately gives them the strength to begin walking on his or her own. We must be committed not only to seeing people born-again, but also to discipling them such that they become strong in the Lord!

Acts 13:22...A Man After God's Own Heart

Acts 13:22 and I Samuel 13:14 both describe David as being a man after God's own heart. I Samuel declares, "....the Lord hath sought him a man after his own heart." The Hebrew word translated "after" is *achar*, and the Greek word translated "after" is *kata*. The meaning of *achar* is "following after or pursuing" as opposed to the meaning of *kata*, which is "in the likeness of." The principle meaning of this word is not that David's heart was so pure, wonderful, and glorious like God's heart, but rather, he was <u>seeking after</u> the heart of God.

Acts 28:1-5...Shake the Serpent into the Fire

Acts 28 records the account of Paul on the Isle of Melita after he was shipwrecked. He was there with the other shipwrecked passengers as well as the natives, and they were building a fire to warm themselves and dry out. A viper came out of the fire and fastened itself to Paul's hand. Why did the serpent attach itself to his hand? I believe it's because Paul's healing hands were the instruments that God was going to use to bring revival to the island. Satan always attacks that of which he is most fearful. Acts 28:5 states, "And he shook off the beast into the fire, and felt no harm."

We can compare this verse to Revelation 20:10, which effectively says that Satan is going to be shaken off into the Lake of Fire. I believe we are going to have the privilege of witnessing the final "shake and bake" ceremony. That old serpent is not going to win!

I Corinthians 9:25-27...Out to Pasture

This is a sobering warning as Paul writes to the church at Corinth about running the race in a way so as to receive the prize. Verse 25 states, "And every man that striveth for the mastery is temperate in all things. Now they do it to obtain a corruptible crown; but we an incorruptible. I therefore so run, not as uncertainly; so fight I, not as one that beateth the air. But I keep under my body, and bring it into subjection; lest that by any means, when I have preached to others, I myself should be a castaway."

That word "castaway" is translated from the Greek word *adokimos*, which means "worthless, rejected, disqualified, or unapproved." It does not mean "destroyed!" It is like a horse being put out to pasture after he can no longer endure the demands placed upon him in the race. God, in His mercy, may put a man out to pasture, but He doesn't destroy him. I suppose there is not one of us that haven't felt the sting of failure and the pain of saying, "Lord I was wrong." In those cases, God may take us out of the race for awhile, but He won't destroy us!

Ephesians 4:15-16...Every Joint Supplies

Paul paints a powerful picture of the spiritual body, the Body of Christ when he writes, speaking of Christ, in Ephesians 4:16, "From whom the whole body fitly joined together..." Paul was effectively saying that it is Christ that determines the location, virtue, and if there be any praise, think on these things."

It is important to realize that the conjunction that ties the list of these things together is not the word "<u>or</u>" but the word "<u>and</u>." Therefore, in order for something to pass the test of being acceptable to think or speak about, it should meet <u>all</u> of the criteria. It should not only be true but also honest, just, pure, lovely, of good report, virtuous, <u>and</u> be of praise. That's quite a heavy test. I used to try to challenge people about saying certain things, and they might respond, "But it's true!" However, even if what they are saying is true, perhaps it isn't pure, just, lovely, etc... We must evaluate all of the criteria before thinking or speaking. The conjunction <u>and</u> is the key word!

Philippians 4:11-19...Christ's Strength and Supply

"Not that I speak in respect of want; for I have learned, in whatsoever state I am, therewith to be content. I know both how to be abased, and I know how to abound every where and in all things I am instructed both to be full and to be hungry, both to abound and to suffer need. I can do all things through Christ which strengtheneth me."

We cannot separate verse 13 from verses 11 and 12. I've seen people that thought they could jump off a twelve story building because of verse 13, but that is not what the Bible is saying. Paul was effectively saying that we can do any of <u>these things</u>

through the strength of Christ. What things? What does Christ give us the strength to do? Christ gives us the strength to be abased and still serve God and the strength to abound and still serve God. Whether full or hungry, abounding or suffering need, Christ gives us the strength to be content in every situation!

The context is also very important in Philippians 4:14-19 where Paul is writing to the church, "Notwithstanding ye have well done, that ye did communicate with my affliction. Now ye Philippians know also, that in the beginning of the gospel, when I departed from Macedonia, no church communicated with me as concerning giving and receiving, but ye only. For even in Thessalonica ye sent once and again unto my necessity. Not because I desire a gift; but I desire fruit that may abound to your account. But I have all, and abound; I am full, having received of Epaphroditus the things which were sent from you, an odour of a sweet smell, a sacrifice acceptable, well-pleasing to God. But my God shall supply all your need according to his riches in glory by Christ Jesus."

Philippians 4:19, in the original text, says "And" not "But." That means that God is continuing the flow of thought from the proceeding verses, and we just can't quote Philippians 4:19 as a standalone verse. It must be interpreted in the context in which it is found, and when interpreted in its context, Paul is effectively saying, "Because of your generosity to me, God will supply all of your needs."

Colossians 1:12-13...Darkness and Light

Colossians 1:12-13 declares, "Giving thanks unto the Father, which hath made us meet to be partakers of the inheritance of the saints in <u>light</u>. Who hath delivered us from the power of <u>darkness</u>, and hath translated us into the kingdom of his dear Son;"

We are children of the light, not of the darkness. We are children of the day, not of the night. God always intervenes in times of darkness; in places of darkness He brings light because He is a God of light, a God that reveals light, and a God that <u>is</u> light. Jesus said "I am the light of the world" (John 9:5) and He said of us that we are the light of the world. (Matthew 5:14)

II Timothy 3:12...Suffering Persecution

Paul in writing to Timothy, his young son in the faith, wrote, "Yea, and all that will live godly in Christ Jesus shall suffer persecution." (II Timothy 3:12) I encourage you that if you are not experiencing persecution, don't boast about it, because everyone that lives godly will experience persecution at one time or another.

II Timothy 4:7...I Have Finished My Course

I love the final testimony of the Apostle Paul, which he wrote near the end of his life to his spiritual son Timothy, whom he mentored in the Lord, "I have fought a good fight, I have finished my course, I have kept the faith;" (II Timothy 4:7)

The word translated "finished" is the Greek word *teleo*. It's a different Greek word than *sumbibazo* although it is also translated "finished" in some places. There is a difference between the two words that is very significant. The word *teleo* means "completed, finished, accomplished, and fully carried out." It is the word Jesus used on the cross when He said, "It is finished." He was effectively saying, "I have fully carried out, accomplished, and brought to perfection everything I was called to do."

In contrast, the Greek word *sumbibazo* simply means "ended, concluded, over, done, or expired." We can be "done" without being "finished." There is a difference! I believe that the Apostle Paul, just like Jesus, knew in his spirit that he had completed everything he was sent to do. There is a deep sense of satisfaction and fulfillment, of laying something at Jesus' feet and knowing we have done everything we have known to do, and obeyed everything we have heard Him tell us to do. I pray that each of us reaches that point at the end of our lives.

Dr. Leonard Gardner

Hebrews 8:5...Go to the Mount

The writer of Hebrews speaks of striving for a higher level of ministry in pleasing God and being effective in His service, when he writes, "Who serve unto the example and shadow of heavenly things, as Moses was admonished of God when he was about to make the tabernacle; for See, saith he, that thou make all things according to the pattern shewed to thee in the mount." (Hebrews 8:5)

God's word to Moses was therefore, "...make all things according to the pattern shewed to thee in the mount." The word translated "pattern" is the Greek word *tupos*, which means "model" or "sample." In order to move in obedience to God's will, we must spend time "in the mount." Going to the mount means getting into God's presence, seeking Him with an open heart and mind, and being willing to do and be what He would have us do and be. When we do that, He will give us direction, and the blessing comes not in doing something that worked for someone else, but rather doing what the Lord tells each of us to do individually and specifically.

Many decades ago, we planted a church with just five people. Over the course of time, by God's grace, we started growing, and I began to receive telephone calls from people asking what I had done to make the church grow. I think I disappointed them when I said, "I simply obeyed what God told me to do." There is no formula or template that fits all of us. There is no shortcut for going to the mount and seeking God for ourselves.

God blesses obedience. We can preach and sing about His Lordship until we are hoarse, but the highest order of recognizing His Lordship is obeying Him. Mary clearly illustrated this when she said, "Whatsoever he saith unto thee do it." (John 2:5) God blesses obedience! It's not in a "one size fits all" formula. It's in obedience to what He specifically said to you.

The children of Israel effectively said to Moses, go to the mountain and find out what God is saying." The Israelites effectively said, "God is too awesome. We have been slaves for four hundred years. Slaves can't approach a holy God. Moses, go talk to Him on our behalf and tell us what He says." However, God's eternal purpose was never to have a company of priests or intermediaries to interact with Him on behalf of the people. His purpose was to have every single one of His people be "priests" in the sense that they can approach Him and hear His direction for themselves. God is bringing us, as His universal church, to that point through Christ. I Peter 2:9 declares that we are each to be priests! Therefore, we can each go to the mount, get into God's presence, and hear from Him ourselves concerning the things He would have us do. And then, we must obey everything He says, and His blessing will surely follow!

Hebrews 8:12...He Chooses Not to Remember

I have heard it said that God "forgives and forgets," but that is not scriptural. Hebrews 8:12 declares, "For I will be merciful to their unrighteousness, and their sins and their iniquities will I remember no more."

There is a difference between choosing to remember no more as opposed to forgetting. To forget something implies a loss of ability or control, and God never loses control. He is omniscient and therefore knows everything about all things at all times. Therefore, as an expression of His mercy, grace, and love, He <u>chooses not to remember</u>. He chooses not to do what He could do, and that shows how much He loves us. The God we serve doesn't forget - He forgives. He "remembers no more." What a wonderful, glorious, faithful God we serve!

About the Author

Blessed with the caring, compassionate heart of a shepherd, Dr. Leonard Gardner has over 60 years of pastoral and ministerial experience. Often called a "pastor's pastor," he has planted churches and mentored pastors and leaders in the true spirit of a "father." Dr. Gardner is the founder of Liberating Word Ministries (www.liberatingword.org) and he travels throughout the United States and abroad with a vision to strengthen and encourage pastors, leaders, churches, and ministries. His heart is for restoration and revival. His style of ministry is seasoned with humor while carrying a powerful anointing. Dr. Gardner has four children and resides in Clinton Township, Michigan.

More Inspirational Books from Dr. Leonard Gardner

Eight Principles of Abundant Living

In this inspiring and thought provoking book, Pastor Gardner examines each recorded miracle in the Book of John to uncover spiritual principles of abundant living which can lead you into a lifestyle of deep satisfaction, joy, fulfillment, and true happiness.

The Unfeigned Love of God

The Bible uses the word "unfeigned" to characterize the indescribable love of God. Unfeigned means "genuine, real, pure, not pretentious, and not hypocritical." This powerful book, derived from a series of sermons by Pastor Gardner, will help you understand, accept, and embrace the incredible love God seeks to lavish on you.

Walking Through the High and Hard Places

Life has its ups and downs. The key to a fulfilling life is learning to "walk through" whatever situation or circumstance you encounter, and to emerge victoriously! The spiritual principles you learn in this book will give you the strength to handle any circumstance in life!

The Work of the Potter's Hands

You are not alive by accident! Isaiah 64:8 declares that God is the potter, and we are the clay. This book examines seven types of Biblical pottery vessels and the process the potter uses to shape and repair vessels. Learn powerful life lessons and know your life is in the hands of a loving God who is forming you through life's experiences so that you "take shape" to fulfill your unique purpose.

It's All in the Blood

This fascinating book draws intriguing and powerful analogies between the incredible design and operation of blood in the human body, and the life-changing spiritual power and provision that is available in the blood of Jesus Christ.

Like the Eagle

Learn how the eagle's lifestyle and attributes can teach you to "soar higher" in your life, as you become like the eagle in areas such as vision, diet, maturity, renewal, commitment, and living an overcoming life.

The Blood Covenant

Blood covenant is a central theme of the entire Bible, and understanding blood covenant will make the Bible come alive to you in brand new ways. Learn the ten steps of blood covenant, the real significance of communion, the names of God and what they mean, and how walking in a true covenant relationship with God can radically change your life.

Bread that Satisfies

Are you truly satisfied in life? Is your appetite for God everything you desire it to be? The aroma of freshly baked homemade bread awakens hunger in almost anyone. Learn how to stir a similar spiritual hunger in your heart for Jesus, the Bread of Life. Knowing Him will satisfy the deepest hunger of your spirit.

Living in the Favor of God

Is your life is truly blessed? In this study of the Beatitudes, you will learn what Jesus meant by the phrase, "Blessed are they…" Learn the conditions of God's favor as well as the provisions that He has in store for those that desire to truly live a blessed life.

Chosen to Follow Jesus

Who were the twelve disciples? Why did Jesus choose them to follow Him, and what can we learn from their lives? This study of "the twelve" delivers fresh insight into their unique backgrounds and characteristics, and teaches principles that we, as those chosen to follow Jesus today, can apply to our walk with Him.

Liberating Word Ministries

PO Box 380291
Clinton Township, MI 48038
Phone: (586) 216-3668
Fax: (586) 416-4658
lgardner@liberatingword.org

www.liberatingword.org

Made in the USA
Charleston, SC
07 December 2012